Collins Revised

Engaging English 3

Ruby Bose

Components of DigiSuite

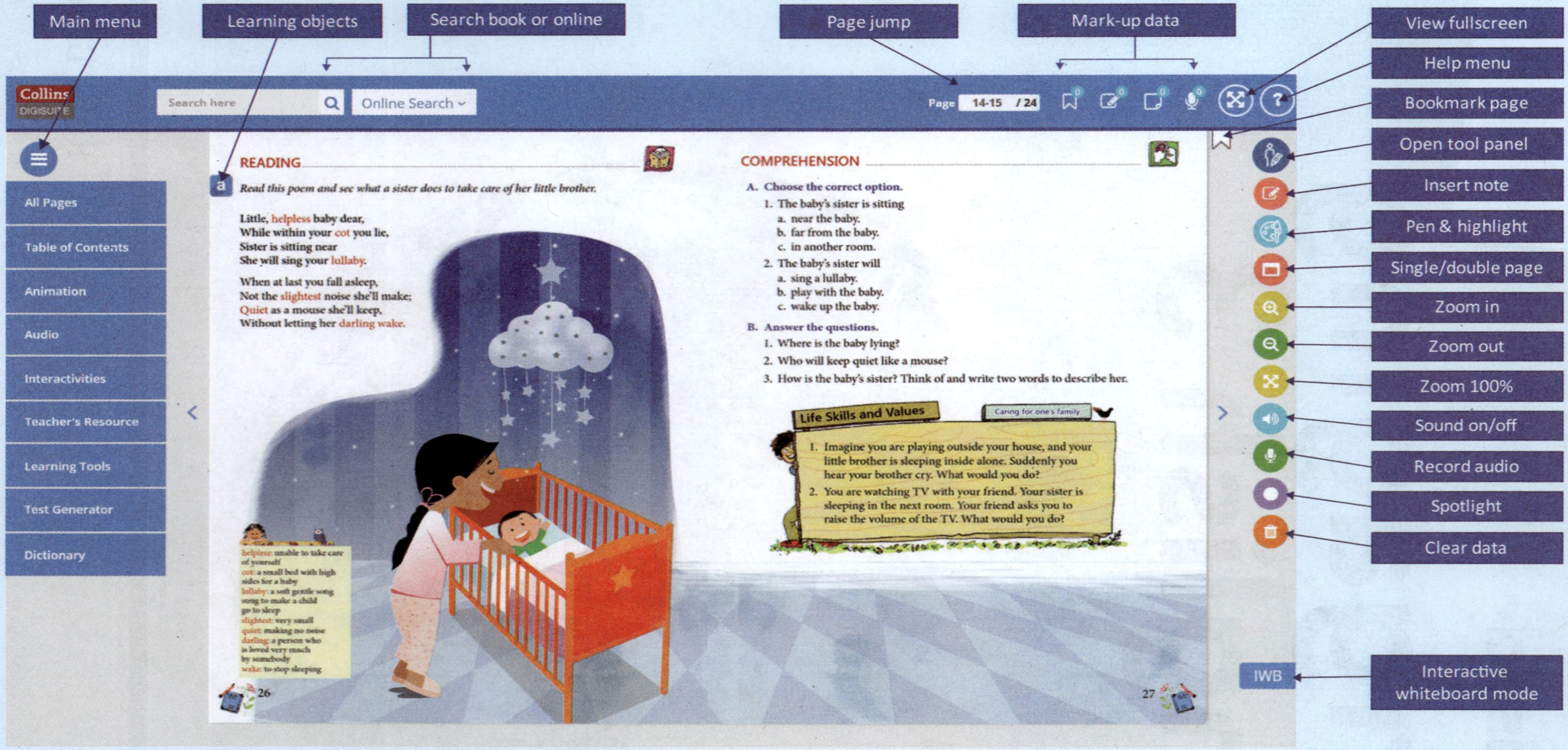

Student + Teacher			Teacher-only	
a animations	**ia** activities	**g** games	**lp** lesson plans	**tn** teacher's notes
ilt instructor-led tutorials	**w** worksheets	**v** videos	**w** worksheets	**ak** answer keys
	audio			

Preface

Revised Engaging English aims to instill an appreciation for literature in today's learners, while equipping them with the tools to develop native fluency and communicative competence in using the English language.

This eight-level series has been designed to teach language skills through the use of literature. Comprising Coursebooks and Workbooks, and digital resources for teachers for all levels, the series is meant to be educative as well as inspiring, imparting moral values and arousing the learner's curiosity about the world beyond the classroom.

In the revised edition, the series has been aligned closely with the guidelines of the National Education Policy, 2020 through its focus on twenty-first century skills, Sustainable Development Goals (SDGs), cross-curricular learning, 'Happiness' content and art-integrated learning. Coursebooks 1 and 2 integrate the essence of NIPUN (National Initiative for Proficiency in Reading with Understanding and Numeracy), which deals with Foundational Literacy and Numeracy. They aim to motivate students to read independently, improve their vocabulary, develop their critical thinking and creative skills and enhance their ability to express themselves verbally and in writing.

The lessons are built around carefully selected literary pieces with distinct cross-curricular themes, and presented with glossary, explanation of literary terms and interesting trivia. The end-of-chapter exercises address the needs of formal language learning and cover all aspects of language acquisition. They include *Comprehension, Way with Words, Grammar in Use, Study Skills, Listening and Speaking* and *Pen it Down*.

New Features in the Revised Edition

Let's Get Started: A theme-based, cross-curricular warm-up task at the beginning of each lesson spanning subjects like science, history and general knowledge, with a focus on SDGs.

Graphic stories: These include both fiction and non-fiction and address the needs of visual learners.

Cross-curricular trivia: This includes **Did You Know?**, which has interesting information covering science, mathematics, geography, history and general knowledge, related to the passage.

In-text questions: These assess while-reading comprehension of the learner.

Life Skills and Values: A part of Comprehension, this includes questions that encourage learners to think analytically and write creatively, thus building higher order thinking skills. They are aligned to the twenty-first century skills.

Augmented scaffolding: This comprises more detailed explanations for every section, including Way with Words and Grammar in Use. Concepts are presented through graphic organizers and reinforced through practice and repetition. Support is provided for the Listening and Speaking and Pen it Down tasks in the form of suggested points as well as useful words and phrases to facilitate competency-based learning.

Now I can: This is a learner-centric self-assessment checklist of the learning objectives for every lesson.

Be Creative!/Research and Write: These special pages, of which there are three in each book, include several new research-based literary projects, creative writing and vocabulary tasks which revisit the themes of the lessons. These focus variously on art integration and SDGs and support inquiry-based learning.

The **Workbooks** complement the Coursebooks by providing additional skills practice through the careful mapping of grammar and vocabulary. Each Workbook from Classes 3 to 8 includes a test paper based on the principle of SAFAL (Structured Assessment For Analyzing Learning), a competency-based assessment introduced by CBSE in keeping with the guidelines of the NEP. They focus on assessing the competencies of critical thinking as well as inquiry-based and analysis-based learning.

The series is supported with **Teacher's Resource Books** and **Digital resources**.

The series encourages competency-based education which allows concept acquisition at the learner's own pace, based on individual ability. We hope that it will foster a love for literature and reading in young learners.

Author

Ruby Bose has been teaching English for more than a decade at The Heritage School, Kolkata.

Key Features

Let's Get Started

- Theme-based warm-up activities, with a focus on Sustainable Development Goals

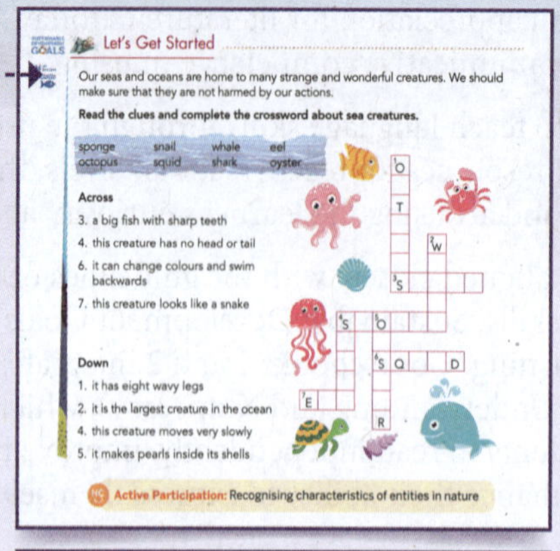

Let's Get Started

Our seas and oceans are home to many strange and wonderful creatures. We should make sure that they are not harmed by our actions.

Read the clues and complete the crossword about sea creatures.

sponge snail whale eel octopus squid shark oyster

Across

3. a big fish with sharp teeth
4. this creature has no head or tail
6. it can change colours and swim backwards
7. this creature looks like a snake

Down

1. it has eight wavy legs
2. it is the largest creature in the ocean
4. this creature moves very slowly
5. it makes pearls inside its shells

Active Participation: Recognising characteristics of entities in nature

Reading

- Has a rich variety of reading passages, including prose, poetry and drama
- Covers literary genres like short stories, biographies, folktales, fables, fantasy, science fiction, non-fiction, extracts from contemporary and classic works, taken from Indian and world literature

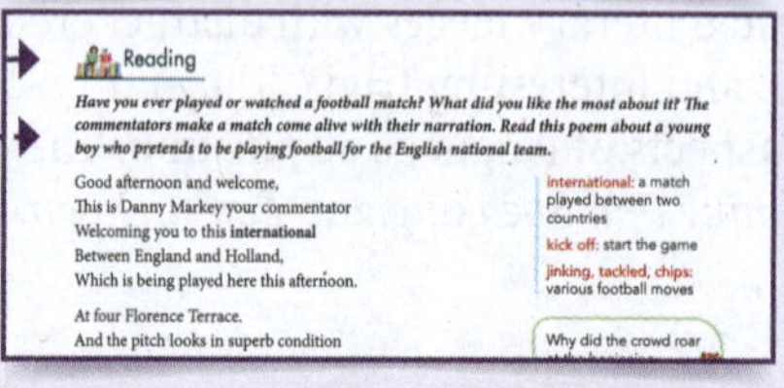

Reading

Have you ever played or watched a football match? What did you like the most about it? The commentators make a match come alive with their narration. Read this poem about a young boy who pretends to be playing football for the English national team.

Good afternoon and welcome,
This is Danny Markey your commentator
Welcoming you to this **international**
Between England and Holland,
Which is being played here this afternoon.

At four Florence Terrace,
And the pitch looks in superb condition

international: a match played between two countries
kick off: start the game
jinking, tackled, chips: various football moves

Why did the crowd roar

Introduction

- Includes background information about the reading text to initiate learners into the passage

Wordwise

- Provides additional information on the origin of words to interest learners in the nuances of language and to improve vocabulary

In-text questions

- 'while-reading' questions to check textual understanding

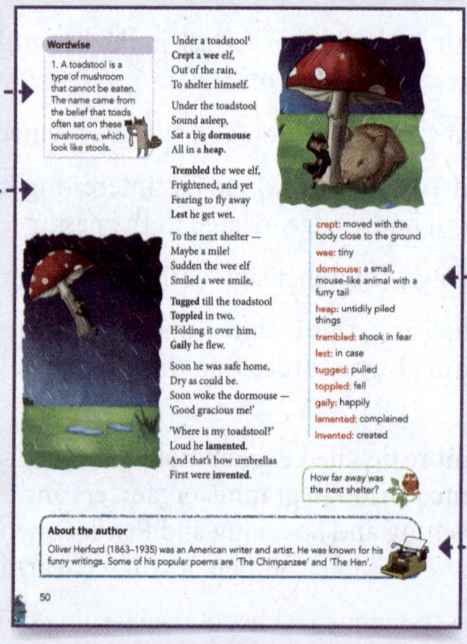

Wordwise

1. A toadstool is a type of mushroom that cannot be eaten. The name came from the belief that toads often sat on these mushrooms, which look like stools.

Under a toadstool[1]
Crept a wee elf,
Out of the rain,
To shelter himself.

Under the toadstool
Sound asleep,
Sat a big **dormouse**
All in a **heap**.

Trembled the wee elf,
Frightened, and yet
Fearing to fly away
Lest he get wet.

To the next shelter —
Maybe a mile!
Sudden the wee elf
Smiled a wee smile,

Tugged till the toadstool
Toppled in two.
Holding it over him,
Gaily he flew.

Soon he was safe home,
Dry as could be.
Soon woke the dormouse —
'Good gracious me!'

'Where is my toadstool?'
Loud he **lamented**.
And that's how umbrellas
First were **invented**.

crept: moved with the body close to the ground
wee: tiny
dormouse: a small, mouse-like animal with a furry tail
heap: untidily piled things
trembled: shook in fear
lest: in case
tugged: pulled
toppled: fell
gaily: happily
lamented: complained
invented: created

How far away was the next shelter?

About the author

Oliver Herford (1863–1935) was an American writer and artist. He was known for his funny writings. Some of his popular poems are 'The Chimpanzee' and 'The Hen'.

50

Comprehension

- 'Quick Recap' checks factual understanding through 'who', 'what', 'where', and 'how' questions; also includes 'reference to context' questions to test in-depth understanding of the lesson

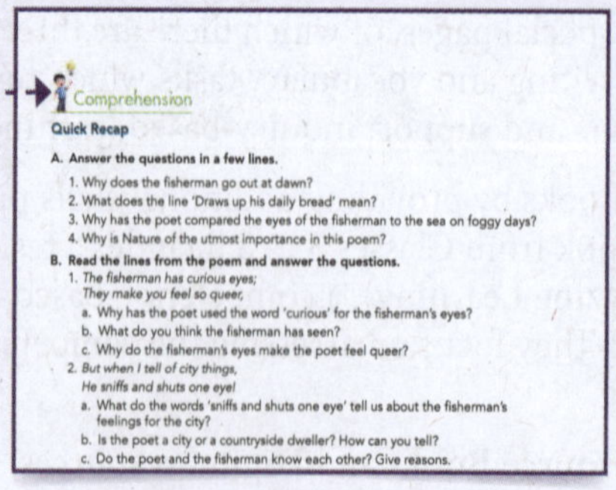

Comprehension

Quick Recap

A. Answer the questions in a few lines.

1. Why does the fisherman go out at dawn?
2. What does the line 'Draws up his daily bread' mean?
3. Why has the poet compared the eyes of the fisherman to the sea on foggy days?
4. Why is Nature of the utmost importance in this poem?

B. Read the lines from the poem and answer the questions.

1. *The fisherman has curious eyes;*
   They make you feel so queer,
   a. Why has the poet used the word 'curious' for the fisherman's eyes?
   b. What do you think the fisherman has seen?
   c. Why do the fisherman's eyes make the poet feel queer?
2. *But when I tell of city things,*
   He sniffs and shuts one eye!
   a. What do the words 'sniffs and shuts one eye' tell us about the fisherman's feelings for the city?
   b. Is the poet a city or a countryside dweller? How can you tell?
   c. Do the poet and the fisherman know each other? Give reasons.

Life Skills and Values

- Inferential and extrapolative higher order thinking skills (HOTS) questions on moral values and interpersonal skills, mapped to twenty-first century skills

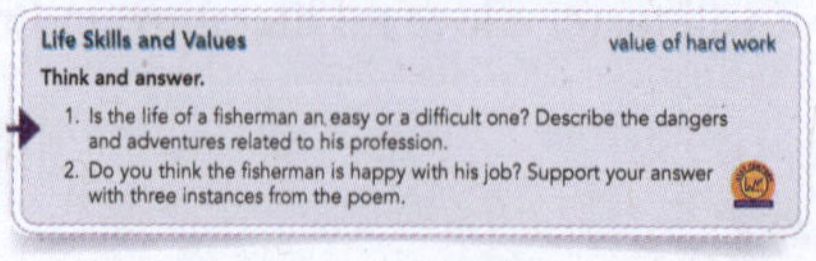

Life Skills and Values value of hard work

Think and answer.

1. Is the life of a fisherman an easy or a difficult one? Describe the dangers and adventures related to his profession.
2. Do you think the fisherman is happy with his job? Support your answer with three instances from the poem.

Graphic Story

- Graphic story in Classes 1-7 to aid visual learning

Glossary

- Provides contextual meanings of difficult words and phrases, given alongside the reading passage

About the author/poet

- Gives a brief biography of the writer, with names of their best known works

Literary term, Did You Know?

- Provide additional information on literary devices and figures of speech, and trivia to develop cross-curricular intelligence

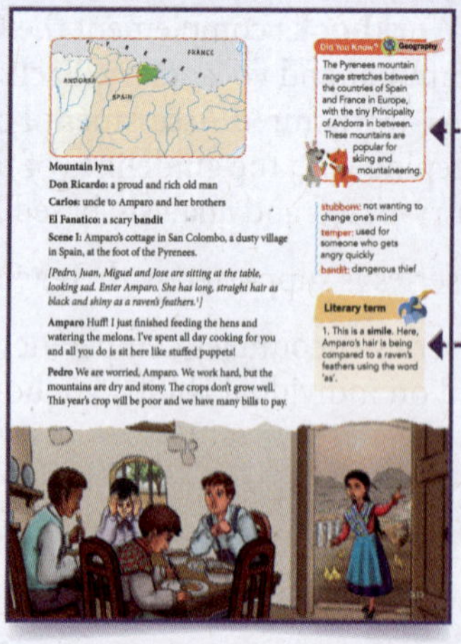

Did You Know? Geography

The Pyrenees mountain range stretches between the countries of Spain and France in Europe, with the tiny Principality of Andorra in between. These mountains are popular for skiing and mountaineering.

Mountain lynx
Don Ricardo: a proud and rich old man
Carlos: uncle to Amparo and her brothers
El Fanatico: a scary bandit

Scene I: Amparo's cottage in San Colombo, a dusty village in Spain, at the foot of the Pyrenees.

[Pedro, Juan, Miguel and Jose are sitting at the table, looking sad. Enter Amparo. She has long, straight hair as black and shiny as a raven's feathers.]

Amparo Huff! I just finished feeding the hens and watering the melons. I've spent all day cooking for you and all you do is sit here like stuffed puppets!

Pedro We are worried, Amparo. We work hard, but the mountains are dry and stony. The crops don't grow well. This year's crop will be poor and we have many bills to pay.

stubborn: not wanting to change one's mind
temper: used for someone who gets angry quickly
bandit: dangerous thief

Literary term

1. This is a simile. Here, Amparo's hair is being compared to a raven's feathers using the word 'as'.

Way with Words

- Includes exercises on contextual application of language encountered in the reading text
- Fosters appreciation of literary devices and figures of speech (simile, metaphor, personification, etc)

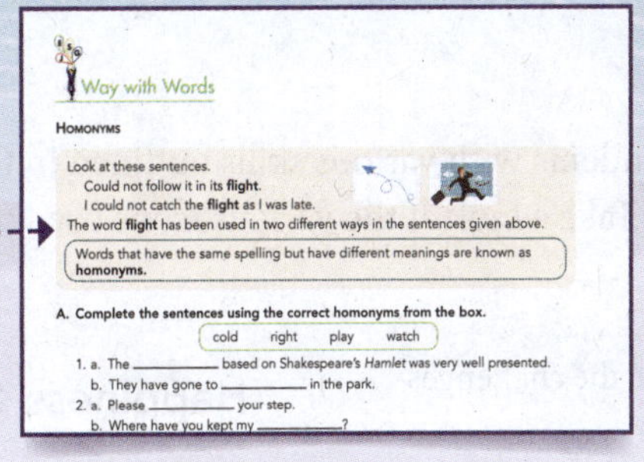
Way with Words

HOMONYMS

Look at these sentences.
Could not follow it in its **flight**.
I could not catch the **flight** as I was late.
The word **flight** has been used in two different ways in the sentences given above.

Words that have the same spelling but have different meanings are known as **homonyms**.

A. Complete the sentences using the correct homonyms from the box.

cold | right | play | watch

1. a. The ________ based on Shakespeare's *Hamlet* was very well presented.
b. They have gone to ________ in the park.
2. a. Please ________ your step.
b. Where have you kept my ________?

Grammar in Use

- Imparts formal understanding of language structures and syntax
- Includes easy-to-understand explanations of grammar concepts, graphic organisers and plenty of practice exercises

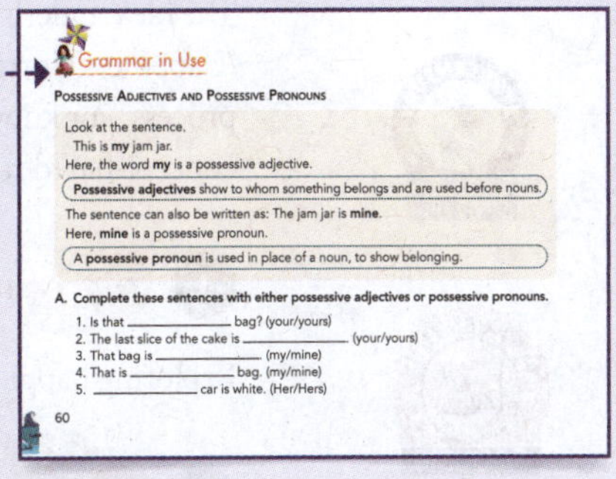
Grammar in Use

POSSESSIVE ADJECTIVES AND POSSESSIVE PRONOUNS

Look at the sentence.
This is **my** jam jar.
Here, the word **my** is a possessive adjective.

Possessive adjectives show to whom something belongs and are used before nouns.

The sentence can also be written as: The jam jar is **mine**.
Here, **mine** is a possessive pronoun.

A possessive pronoun is used in place of a noun, to show belonging.

A. Complete these sentences with either possessive adjectives or possessive pronouns.

1. Is that ________ bag? (your/yours)
2. The last slice of the cake is ________ (your/yours)
3. That bag is ________ (my/mine)
4. That is ________ bag. (my/mine)
5. ________ car is white. (Her/Hers)

60

Listening and Speaking

- Facilitates fluency in oral and aural communication
- Includes conversation practice, role plays, debates and listening comprehension
- Exercises on rhyme and meter in poetry chapters

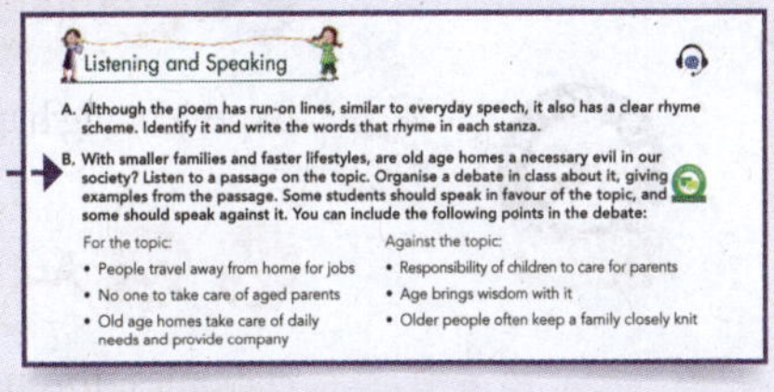
Listening and Speaking

A. Although the poem has run-on lines, similar to everyday speech, it also has a clear rhyme scheme. Identify it and write the words that rhyme in each stanza.

B. With smaller families and faster lifestyles, are old age homes a necessary evil in our society? Listen to a passage on the topic. Organise a debate in class about it, giving examples from the passage. Some students should speak in favour of the topic, and some should speak against it. You can include the following points in the debate:

For the topic:
- People travel away from home for jobs
- No one to take care of aged parents
- Old age homes take care of daily needs and provide company

Against the topic:
- Responsibility of children to care for parents
- Age brings wisdom with it
- Older people often keep a family closely knit

Pen it Down

- Includes guided and free writing tasks, to enable learners to express themselves creatively, logically and coherently

Now I can

- Self-assessment of learning objectives for the chapter

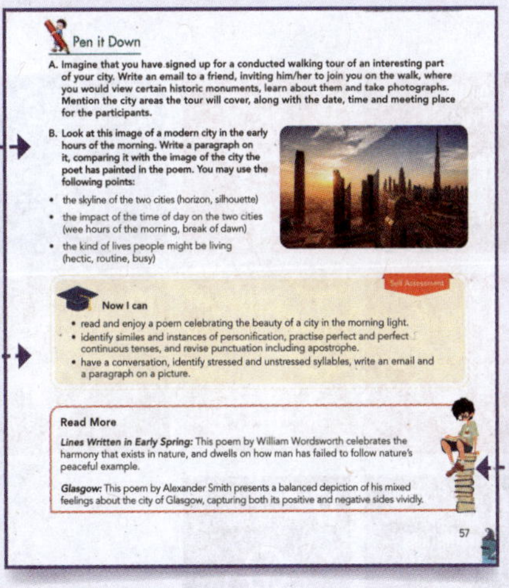
Pen it Down

A. Imagine that you have signed up for a conducted walking tour of an interesting part of your city. Write an email to a friend, inviting him/her to join you on the walk, where you would view certain historic monuments, learn about them and take photographs. Mention the city areas the tour will cover, along with the date, time and meeting place for the participants.

B. Look at this image of a modern city in the early hours of the morning. Write a paragraph on it, comparing it with the image of the city the poet has painted in the poem. You may use the following points:

- the skyline of the two cities (horizon, silhouette)
- the impact of the time of day on the two cities (wee hours of the morning, break of dawn)
- the kind of lives people might be living (hectic, routine, busy)

Self Assessment

Now I can
- read and enjoy a poem celebrating the beauty of a city in the morning light.
- identify similes and instances of personification, practise perfect and perfect continuous tenses, and revise punctuation including apostrophe.
- have a conversation, identify stressed and unstressed syllables, write an email and a paragraph on a picture.

Read More

Lines Written in Early Spring: This poem by William Wordsworth celebrates the harmony that exists in nature, and dwells on how man has failed to follow nature's peaceful example.

Glasgow: This poem by Alexander Smith presents a balanced depiction of his mixed feelings about the city of Glasgow, capturing both its positive and negative sides vividly.

57

Study Skills

- Develops the sub-skills of language study
- **Spell Check** and **Pronounce Well** include phonics drills and exercises on spelling
- **Use Your Dictionary** develops dictionary referencing skills

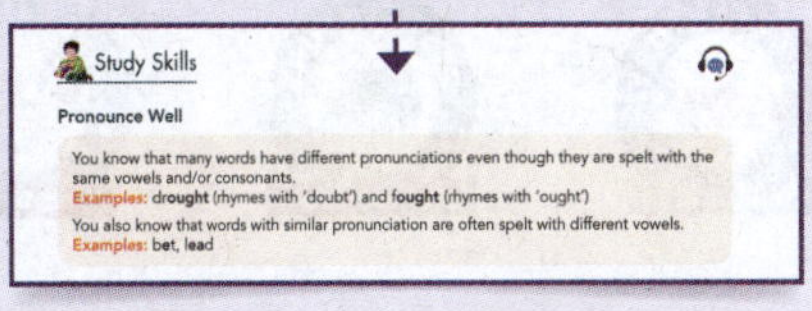
Study Skills

Pronounce Well

You know that many words have different pronunciations even though they are spelt with the same vowels and/or consonants.
Examples: drought (rhymes with 'doubt') and fought (rhymes with 'ought')
You also know that words with similar pronunciation are often spelt with different vowels.
Examples: bet, lead

Literary Genres and Terms

- Includes a glossary to introduce literary genres and explain literary devices and narrative tools

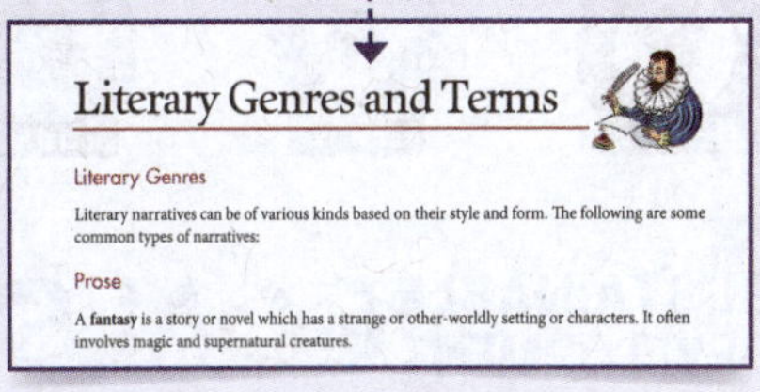
Literary Genres and Terms

Literary Genres

Literary narratives can be of various kinds based on their style and form. The following are some common types of narratives:

Prose

A **fantasy** is a story or novel which has a strange or other-worldly setting or characters. It often involves magic and supernatural creatures.

Read More

- Contains extra suggested reading for the avid learner to foster love for literature

Assessments

- Includes a Test Paper in Workbooks 3-8 based on the principle of SAFAL that encourages competency-based learning

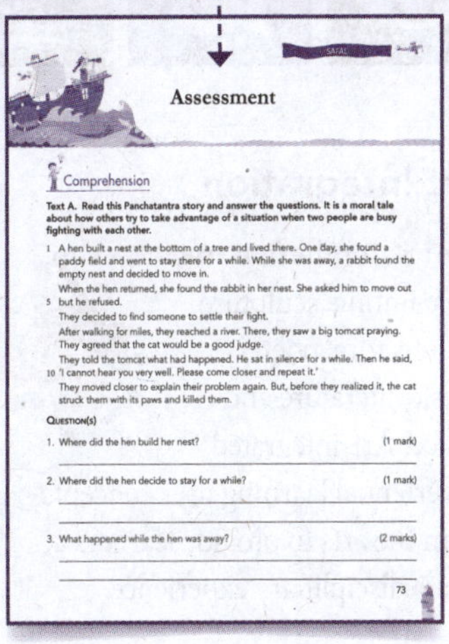
Assessment

Comprehension

Text A. Read this Panchatantra story and answer the questions. It is a moral tale about how others try to take advantage of a situation when two people are busy fighting with each other.

A hen built a nest at the bottom of a tree and lived there. One day, she found a paddy field and went to stay there for a while. While she was away, a rabbit found the empty nest and decided to move in.
When the hen returned, she found the rabbit in her nest. She asked him to move out but he refused.
They decided to find someone to settle their fight.
After walking for miles, they reached a river. There, they saw a big tomcat praying. They agreed that the cat would be a good judge.
They told the tomcat what had happened. He sat in silence for a while. Then he said, 'I cannot hear you very well. Please come closer and repeat it.'
They moved closer to explain their problem again. But, before they realized it, the cat struck them with its paws and killed them.

Question(s)

1. Where did the hen build her nest? (1 mark)
2. Where did the hen decide to stay for a while? (1 mark)
3. What happened while the hen was away? (2 marks)

73

Poster

- Literature and vocabulary games, and activities based on distinct themes

Icons

Revised Engaging English aims to equip students with various skills outlined in the National Education Policy, 2020, that target the holistic education of the learner. Take a look at the various icons used to showcase these skills.

Twenty-first Century Skills

Mastering these skills will equip learners to face the challenges of a rapidly changing, digital society.

21ST CENTURY Collaboration | 21ST CENTURY Communication | 21ST CENTURY Creativity | 21ST CENTURY Critical Thinking

21ST CENTURY Initiative | 21ST CENTURY Leadership | 21ST CENTURY Media Literacy | 21ST CENTURY Productivity

21ST CENTURY Flexibility | 21ST CENTURY Information Literacy | 21ST CENTURY Social Skills | 21ST CENTURY Technology Literacy

Happiness Content

The idea underlying 'Happiness Content', a part of the 'Happiness Curriculum', is that learning should be an enjoyable process. For knowledge to bring joy, learning must focus on concept-based rather than rote learning.

1 HC **Learning and Awareness**

Exploring happiness through Learning and Awareness

2 HC **Feelings**

Experiencing happiness in relationships through Feelings

3 HC **Active Participation**

Happiness through Active Participation

SUSTAINABLE DEVELOPMENT GOALS

1 NO POVERTY | 2 ZERO HUNGER | 3 GOOD HEALTH AND WELL-BEING | 4 QUALITY EDUCATION | 5 GENDER EQUALITY | 6 CLEAN WATER AND SANITATION

7 AFFORDABLE AND CLEAN ENERGY | 8 DECENT WORK AND ECONOMIC GROWTH | 9 INDUSTRY, INNOVATION AND INFRASTRUCTURE | 10 REDUCED INEQUALITIES | 11 SUSTAINABLE CITIES AND COMMUNITIES | 12 RESPONSIBLE CONSUMPTION AND PRODUCTION

13 CLIMATE ACTION | 14 LIFE BELOW WATER | 15 LIFE ON LAND | 16 PEACE, JUSTICE AND STRONG INSTITUTIONS | 17 PARTNERSHIPS FOR THE GOALS

The Sustainable Development Goals (SDGs) were adopted by the United Nations in 2015 as a universal call to action to end poverty, protect the planet, and ensure that by 2030, all people enjoy peace and prosperity. The 17 SDGs recognize that development must balance social, economic and environmental sustainability.

Art Integration

The arts, or the fine arts, are painting, sculpture, architecture, poetry, music, literature and dance. Art-integrated experiential learning uses concepts from the arts to provide learners a multi-disciplinary experience.

ART INTEGRATION

Cross-curricular Content

The cross-curricular approach to teaching recognises that subjects are inter-linked, and for effective concept-acquisition, they must be taught in synergy with each other.

Math

Science

History

Geography

Acknowledgements

The publishers wish to thank and acknowledge the following for granting us permission to use copyright material:

Holiday Activities by Tara Goswami, from *Bogoli Phut Days*, published by HarperCollins India. Reprinted by permission of the author; *The Seed of Truth* by Sudha Murty, from *The Magic Drum*, Puffin Books. Reprinted with the permission of the author; *Breakfast* by Joshua Seigal. Reprinted with the permission of the author; *Anna's Extraordinary Experiments with Weather* (English), written by Nandita Jayaraj, illustrated by Priya Kuriyan, supported by Oracle, published by Pratham Books (© Pratham Books, 2018) under a CC BY 4.0 license on StoryWeaver; *Amparo's Journey* by Gervase Phinn. Reprinted and adapted by permission of the author.

The publishers have applied for permission for the following:
Kangaroos by John Cotton, *Emily's Brush with History* by Ann Schwartz.
Acknowledgements for these texts will be made in the future editions of the book.

Every effort has been made to trace copyright holders and to obtain their permission for the use of copyright material. However, in some instances, we have been unable to trace the owners of the copyright pieces published here. The authors and publishers will gladly receive any information enabling them to rectify any error or omission in subsequent editions.

Illustrations

Inside: Page 6: SDG logo and icons: https://www.un.org/sustainabledevelopment/
The content of this publication has not been approved by the United Nations and does not reflect the views of the United Nations or its officials or Member States. **11:** gerenme, Natalie; **12:** johnwoodcock; **14:** Benjavisa; **15:** Hana Kruzikova; **16:** natsuk; **17:** caraman, mi007; **18:** sabelskaya; **19:** zaricm; **23:** Yudina Anna; **26:** sarno sarno; **27:** dedMazay; **28:** mauribo, Md Sojibul Islam; **32:** stockillustration; **34:** beastfromeast; **39:** Sunnynsk; **41:** MicrovOne; **44:** margouillatphotos; **46:** Onimages; **47:** ajijchan; **48:** kbeis; **49:** zaricm, PANKAJ JAGYA, bordoressam; **53:** kathykonkle; **54:** kristijanh; **55:** INDECcraft, ovchynnikov, girlfrommars; **56:** natapat; **64:** peanutpie; **66:** coffeee-in, viyadaistock; **66:** stock_shoppe; **69:** Galyna; **70:** JakeOlimb; **77:** IconicBestiary; **78:** elenabs; **79:** tachyglossus; **82:** sorbetto; **84:** raclro; **94:** bennymarty, leonello, GlobalP, Freder; **99:** Muhammad Desta Laksana; **100:** Tomacco; **101:** Russelltatedotcom; **103:** Rainer Lesniewski; **104:** Dmitry Volkov; **113:** negoworks; **120:** BraunS, SDI Productions, subodhsathe, OSTILL, DmitryChulov; **124:** GoodStock, Liudmyla Klymenko; **136:** exxorian, colematt; **139:** HelgaMariah; **143:** sabelskaya

Detailed Contents

Unit	Theme	Comprehension	Way with Words	Grammar in Use	Study Skills	Listening and Speaking	Pen it Down
1. A Glass of Milk	Neighbourhood and Community	• Questions • Reference to context	• Contextual usage: fill in the blanks • Anagrams	• Adjectives • Material nouns • Nouns: gender	• Spell Check: *-el* or *-le*	• Conversation: asking for help	• Diary entry using hints
2. A Faithful Act	Friendship and Loyalty	• Questions • Reference to context	• Words related to birds • Binomial pairs	• Collective nouns • Pronouns	• Spell Check: ways of spelling the /f/ sound	• Listening comprehension	• Paragraph writing
3. The Rooks	A Home of One's Own	• Questions • Reference to context	• Animal sounds • Sentence composition • Contextual usage: fill in the blanks	• Tenses: simple past, present and future	• Use Your Dictionary: alphabetical order	• Tongue twisters	• Writing a poem using rhyming words
4. Holiday Activities	India's Northeast	• Fill in the blanks • Questions • Reference to context	• Fruits and Vegetables • Contextual usage: fill in the blanks	• Prepositions of time and place • Comparison of adjectives	• Pronounce Well: words ending with /d/ or /t/ sounds	• Completing a dialogue	• Completing a paragraph
5. The History of Chocolate	Food Around the World	• Questions • Reference to context	• Same words used as different parts of speech • Contextual usage: fill in the blanks	• Question words • Conjunctions	• Pronounce Well: *a* sound	• Listening comprehension: questions	• Picture composition
6. The Elf and the Dormouse	Folktales	• Questions • Reference to context	• Opposite words • Expressions	• Common and proper nouns • Inverted commas	• Use Your Dictionary: finding information using a dictionary	• Narrating an experience	• Paragraph writing
Be Creative!							
7. The Seed of Truth	Tales from India	• Questions • Reference to context	• Proverbs • Scrambled words	• Types of sentences • Definite and indefinite articles	• Spell Check: homophones	• Conversation: speaking on a given topic	• Paragraph writing
8. Breakfast	Health and Nutrition	• Fill in the blanks • Questions • Reference to context	• Contextual usage: fill in the blanks • Words related to taste	• Agreement of subject and verb • Conditional sentences	• Spell Check: commonly confused spellings	• Looking at a picture and describing it	• List making
9. Adventure at the Circus	Family and Friends	• Sequencing • Questions • Reference to context	• Sound words • Movement verbs	• Adverbs	• Pronounce Well: words ending in *-ure*	• Conversation: asking for permission	• Poster making
10. Two Little Kittens	Our Pets	• Reference to context • Questions	• Prefixes: *un, dis, in* • Words related to winter	• Contractions • Negative sentences with *not*	• Use Your Dictionary: multiple meanings of the same word	• Role play	• Letter writing

Unit	Theme	Comprehension	Way with Words	Grammar in Use	Study Skills	Listening and Speaking	Pen it Down
11. Anna's Experiments with Weather	Women in Science	• Completing sentences by choosing correct options • Questions • Reference to context	• Words related to science • Homophones	• Subject and predicate • Pronouns: possessive and demonstrative	• Pronounce Well: /sh/ and /s/ sounds	• Listening comprehension: questions	• Writing a poem
12. Kangaroos	Animals from Down Under	• Completing sentences • Reference to context	• Contextual usage: fill in the blanks • Rhyming words	• Subject, verb, object • Negative contractions	• Spell Check: doubled letters	• Word game	• Writing on a given topic
Be Creative!							
13. Amparo's Journey	Brave Deeds	• Questions • Reference to context	• Phrasal verbs • Suffixes	• Forming the present continuous tense using helping verbs • Prepositional phrases	• Use Your Dictionary: making new words from a given word	• Rising and falling intonation in *wh-* questions	• Paragraph writing
14. The Land of Fib	Space Stories	• Sequencing • Questions • Reference to context	• Professions • Contextual usage: replacing words in sentences	• Past continuous tense • Use of comma	• Use Your Dictionary: finding information about a given word	• Rising intonation in *yes/no* questions • Making a story with given words	• Letter writing
15. The Land of Counterpane	Physical Activities and Sports	• Completing sentences by matching • Reference to context	• Adjectives • Words related to nature • Rhyming words	• Modal verbs • Types of adjectives	• Spell Check: words with *sh* and *ch*	• Listening comprehension: listing plurals	• List making • Rewriting a poem in prose
16. Emily's Brush with History	Ancient History	• Questions • Reference to context	• Compound words • Collocations	• Joining sentences with *who* • Punctuation: capital letters and full stop	• Pronounce Well: different pronunciations of *-ng-*	• Conversation on a given topic	• Paragraph writing
17. An Animal's Prayer	Saving the Environment	• Questions • Reference to context	• Similes • Animals and their young	• Types of adverbs • Apostrophe	• Use Your Dictionary: different meanings of the same word	• Discussion on a given topic	• Dialogue writing
Be Creative!							
Literary Genres and Terms							

Contents

1

A Glass of Milk

Let's Get Started

The United Nations Sustainable Development Goal 2 is about zero hunger. It says that we must try to end hunger from the world through better nutrition.

The Government of India introduced the 'Mid-day Meal Scheme' in schools in 1995 to provide better nutrition to school-going children all over the country. In 2020, when schools were closed due to the coronavirus pandemic, the government delivered food grains or cooked meals to the students' homes in many places.

Imagine that the government has asked you to create a plan for nutritious and tasty meals for children. Make a meal plan for the five days of the school week. Ensure that you include healthy cereals, fruits and vegetables, and milk or yogurt. Do not include unhealthy or expensive food items.

HC **Feelings:** Responsibility towards others

Reading

Do you think that we should help strangers? Would you share something of yours with a stranger if they needed it? Read this story about a poor boy who repays the kindness shown to him many years ago by a girl whom he did not know.

There was once a poor boy who sold **knick-knacks** from door to door to pay for his school fees. One day, he found that he had only a few pennies left. He was very hungry and did not even have the strength to walk a few steps.

He decided that he would ask for food at the next house. He knocked on the door, but lost his **courage** when a young girl came to the doorstep. Instead of a meal, he asked the girl for a glass of water.

But the girl brought him a large glass of milk. 'You look very hungry. Please have the milk,' she said.

He was **astonished** by her kindness. He drank the milk slowly, enjoying the taste.

'How much do I **owe** you for this glass of milk?' he asked after he had finished.

'You don't owe me anything,' she replied. 'Mother has taught us never to take money for kindness.'

'Then I thank you from my heart,' he said.

What did the boy ask for?

knick-knacks: small, decorative objects

courage: (here) confidence

astonished: surprised

owe: to have to pay money to someone

specialist: (here) a doctor who is an expert in treating one type of illness

The boy left with a full belly and a strong belief in the goodness of human beings.

Many years later, the same young girl, who was now a woman, was suffering from an uncommon illness which was difficult to treat. The local doctors did not know what to do. They sent her to a hospital in the big city.

Dr Kevin Bernard, a famous **specialist**, was going to examine her. When he heard the name of the town she was from, a light

Why was the woman sent to the hospital in the city?

filled his eyes. He got up and went down the hospital hall to her room. He entered and recognised her at once. She was the same girl who had given him a glass of milk all those years ago!

She was too ill to remember him. But he was **determined** to do his best to save her. From that day, he gave special attention to the case.

Dr Bernard fought the **disease** for months. At last, he was successful. The woman was completely cured. But she was not rich and was worried about paying the hospital bill.

determined: felt strongly about doing something

disease: illness

cancelled: stopped something that had been planned

How did Dr Bernard react when he heard the name of the town?

Dr Bernard asked the hospital to send the bill to him. He looked at it, wrote a note and sent it to her room along with the bill. The woman was afraid to look at it. She was sure that she would have to spend the rest of her life paying it off.

But when she saw it, her eyes filled with tears of happiness. The bill was **cancelled**. On the note written by Dr Bernard were the words, 'Bill paid years ago with a glass of milk.— Dr Kevin Bernard.'

Comprehension

Quick Recap

A. Answer the questions in a few lines.

1. How did the poor boy earn money?
2. Why did he knock on the girl's door?
3. Why did the girl offer him a glass of milk?
4. Who was Dr Bernard? How did he know the woman?
5. Why was the woman worried about the hospital bill?

B. Read the lines from the story and answer the questions.

1. *'Mother has taught us never to take money for kindness.'*
   a. Who said these words and to whom?
   b. These words were said to answer which question?
   c. What act of kindness had she done?
2. *But when she saw it, her eyes filled with tears of happiness.*
   a. Whose eyes filled with tears of happiness? What did she see?
   b. What had happened to her?
   c. Who had made her happy? How?

Life Skills and Values kindness, gratitude

Think and answer.

1. Why do you think the girl refused to accept money for the glass of milk?
2. Do you think we should repay someone who is kind to us with money alone? How would you repay someone who is kind to you?

Way with Words

A. Complete the sentences with these phrases from the story.

from door to door	lost his courage	from my heart	suffering from	pay it off

1. The businessman had borrowed a lot of money from a friend. He worked hard for a month to __________.

2. I want to thank you ____________ for helping me prepare for my exams.

3. Suman was ____________ chicken pox last summer. So, she could not go out to play.

4. The prince's men went ____________, looking for the owner of the lost shoe.

5. The hunter ____________ when he saw the lion roar and run towards him.

ANAGRAMS

Anagrams are words which can be rearranged to form other words.

Example: earth → heart

B. Rearrange the letters of each word to form words from the story.

1. yob ________	4. tone ________	7. pests ________
2. stare ________	5. tub ________	8. dare ________
3. seam ________	6. dens ________	9. sword ________

Grammar in Use

ADJECTIVES

Read these sentences.

A **young** girl came to the doorstep.

The girl brought him a **large** glass of milk.

The words **young** and **large** are adjectives. **Young** describes the girl. **Large** describes the glass.

Adjectives are describing words. They give us information about a noun or a pronoun in a sentence.

A. Underline the adjectives in these sentences and circle the nouns they describe.

1. Take the new books out of the green bag.

2. Black clouds float across the sky on rainy days.
3. I want to go on the red swing because the blue one is broken.
4. Sneha sat in the first row of the empty classroom and waited for her friends.
5. Can you carry the red suitcase? It is very heavy.
6. The young boy helped the old man cross the busy road.
7. The cow is a domestic animal but the tiger is a wild animal.

Material Nouns

Read these sentences.

The boy decided to ask for **food** at the next house.

The girl brought a large glass of **milk**.

In these sentences, the words **food** and **milk** are names of materials.

Material nouns are names of substances or materials from which things are made.

Examples: cotton, gold, plastic

B. Read these sentences and underline the material nouns.

1. I bought a silk dress yesterday.
2. He is wearing a leather jacket.
3. She is wearing a necklace made of silver.
4. Please serve the ice-creams in glass bowls.
5. Did you know that glass is made of sand?
6. In cold countries, the floors of houses are made of wood.

Nouns: Gender

When nouns refer to males, they are said to be of the **masculine** gender.
Examples: boy, king, lion

When nouns refer to females, they are of the **feminine** gender.
Examples: girl, queen, lioness

Certain nouns refer to both males and females. These are of the **common** gender.
Examples: child, doctor, teacher

Nouns may refer to neither males nor females. Such nouns are of the **neuter** gender.
Examples: glass, milk, bill

C. Change the masculine nouns to feminine nouns and vice versa. Underline the common nouns and circle the neuter nouns.

1. The tiger attacked the bull as it came out of the shed.
2. The witch cast a spell on the princess.
3. The king's nephew became the Prime Minister of the land.
4. The lord loved riding on his white mare.
5. 'Can I speak to my brother, Madam?' the student asked.
6. The monk lived in a cave for years.
7. My uncle bought a new phone.
8. Our landlady lives in the house across the street.

Study Skills

Spell Check

We often confuse the spelling of words which end with **-el** and **-le**, as these letters are often pronounced in the same way.

Look at the way these common **-el** and **-le** words are spelt:

fab**le** ab**le** app**le** chap**el** funn**el**

Complete the words by adding -el or -le.

1. chann______ 3. bott______ 5. hot______ 7. litt______ 9. tunn______
2. pudd______ 4. cam______ 6. trav______ 8. tab______ 10. cand______

Listening and Speaking

Listen to a conversation between a boy who has lost his way and another boy who helps him.

Now, imagine that you have just moved to a new locality. You are looking for a stationery shop where you can buy a notebook. You ask a passerby for help.

Work in pairs and enact the conversation. Use the phrases in the conversation that you have just heard.

HC **Feelings:** Communicating clearly

Pen it Down

Write a diary entry from the young boy's point of view, describing the day the girl offered him a glass of milk. Write in detail about the boy's feelings through his experiences on that day. Use the following hints:

I had not eaten anything – only a few pennies in my pocket – worried about money to pay for my school fees – hungry but too proud to ask a stranger for food – feeling better after drinking the milk – grateful for the girl's kindness – promise to repay her some day

Self Assessment

Now I can

- read about the way people can be kind to us when we don't expect it.
- practise anagrams, identify adjectives, material nouns and the gender of nouns.
- spell words with *-el* and *-le* enact a conversation and write a diary entry.

Read More

Sailor Jim's Telescope: This story from Enid Blyton's *The Secret Door and Other Stories* is about a telescope lent by Sailor Jim to a sick girl as an act of kindness. The telescope later helps the girl save the life of Sailor Jim's mother.

Rikki-Tikki-Tavi: This story from Rudyard Kipling's *The Jungle Book* is about a brave mongoose who saves the human family which had rescued it from a snake.

2

A Faithful Act

Let's Get Started

Do you have a best friend? We can share fun times with friends and ask them for help in difficult situations.

Look at the following situations and write one line each in your notebook about what you would do if you found yourself in them.

1. Your friend is ill and has not been able to attend classes for two weeks. As a result, he/she has missed a lot of classwork and assignments. Your friend is very worried that he/she will do poorly in the upcoming mid-term exams. What do you do?
2. Your best friend rides the bicycle to school every day and follows traffic rules. Someone from your school has complained to your teacher that he/she rode the bike on the wrong side of the road. What do you do?

HC **Learning and Awareness:** Harmony in relationships

Reading

Do you think it is important to be loyal to those whom you love and respect? Read this Jataka tale about a crow who risked his life to fulfil the wish of his queen.

Once upon a time in Kanchanpur, the king of the crows lived with his queen and his **subjects**, a **murder** of crows, on a tree. He loved her very much. One day they flew to the palace of the King of Kanchanpur. The queen crow smelled the deliciously

subjects: those who belong to a country, especially one ruled by a king or a queen

murder: (here) flock

Where did the king of the crows live?

commander: someone in charge of soldiers in an army

perched: (of a bird) landed and sat on something

swoop: fly downwards quickly

Did You Know? History

This is from the *Jataka Tales*, which are stories about the earlier lives of Lord Buddha, in both human and animal forms. Buddha appears in them as a king, a god or as an animal. In every form, he is shown to have certain good qualities.

cooked fish, which the King's cook had made for him. Her mouth watered. But the cook kept a strict eye on the food and she could not steal it. Both returned to their nest.

The next day, the king crow said to his queen, 'Come dear, let us go in search of food.'

'I want the delicious food cooked in the palace or I will kill myself,' cried the queen crow.

What did the queen of the crows threaten to do?

The king wanted to fulfil her wish. He grew thoughtful.

The **commander** of the crows arrived. 'What is the matter, O king? Why do you look worried?' he asked.

When the king told him about the queen's wish, he replied, 'O king, do not be troubled. I will bring the food that the queen wishes to have.'

Soon, flying with eight clever crows, the commander reached the palace of the King of Kanchanpur. They **perched** on the kitchen roof.

The commander said, 'Listen carefully. As soon as the cook comes into the courtyard with the King's food, I will fly to him. I will **swoop** down in such a way that the cook drops the plates. Four of you will fill your beaks with rice and the remaining four will fill your beaks with fish, and fly straight to the queen.'

Soon, the cook came out of the kitchen with the food on a plate. The commander crow swooped down and pecked at his head. The cook dropped the plate in surprise and fear. At the same time, the eight crows flew in, filled their beaks with food and flew away.

'Catch the crow, catch him! Don't let him escape.' the cook shouted. The commander crow had not been as quick as the others. Two soldiers caught him and took him to the King of Kanchanpur. But the crow was not worried.

'Crow, you have put your life in danger by **displeasing** me. Tell me, why did you take such a **risk**?' asked the King.

displeasing: making someone angry

risk: danger that something bad might happen

saluted: showed respect by touching the forehead with one's fingers

Why did the cook drop the plate?

'Our queen wanted to eat the same food that was cooked for you. I promised to get it for her. I have kept my promise. Now, I will accept whatever punishment you give me.'

The King of Kanchanpur was very pleased with the crow's loyalty to his king and queen.

'Such a faithful one should be rewarded and not punished,' he declared. 'Set the crow free. From today, this crow, his king and queen will get a share of the food cooked for me. Rice will be cooked every day for all the other crows too.'

'Thank you, O King. I will always remember your kindness,' said the commander crow.

He **saluted** the King and flew back to his nest.

Why did the commander of the crows thank the King?

Comprehension

Quick Recap

A. Answer the questions in a few lines.

1. Why was the queen crow not able to steal the food cooked for the King of Kanchanpur?
2. How did the commander of the crows plan to steal food from the King's kitchen?
3. Did the commander crow's plan succeed? What happened to him afterwards?
4. How did the King of Kanchanpur treat the commander of the crows?

B. Read the lines from the story and answer the questions.

1. *'What is the matter, O king?'*
   a. Who said these words and to whom?
   b. Why did he ask this question?
   c. What did he promise to do?

2. *'Such a faithful one should be rewarded and not punished.'*
   a. Who said these words?
   b. Who was the 'faithful one'?
   c. Why should he be rewarded?

Life Skills and Values sacrifice, loyalty

Think and answer.

1. Was the king of the crows loved by his murder of crows? How do we know?
2. Do you think the commander acted wisely by trying to steal the food? Give reasons for your answer.
3. Who do you think represents the Buddha in this story? What virtues does he stand for?

Way with Words

Words Related to Birds

The story you just read is about a group of crows and one bird's bravery.

A. Complete the crossword about birds with the help of the clues given.

(Hint: All the words are from the story.)

Across

2. to fly down quickly
4. a common black-coloured bird with a harsh call
5. a bird's mouth

Down

1. moved through the air, using wings
3. sat on a branch

Binomial Pairs

Binomial word pairs show a relationship between two people or groups of people.

Example: king and subjects

B. Complete these word pairs and make sentences with them.

1. buyer and ______________
2. husband and ______________
3. parent and ______________
4. teacher and ______________
5. brother and ______________
6. doctor and ______________

Grammar in Use

Collective Nouns

You know that a noun is a naming word. Nouns can be of various types. Let us look at collective nouns.

Collective nouns are nouns which refer to a group of people, animals or things of the same type.

Examples: a **flock** of birds, a **pride** of lions

A. These collective nouns are jumbled. Rewrite them correctly.

1. A bunch of soldiers ______________
2. An army of players ______________

3. A fleet of students ____________
4. A team of grapes ____________
5. A class of fish ____________
6. A school of ships ____________

PRONOUNS

You have already learned that a pronoun is a word used in place of a noun in a sentence.

Pronouns that are used instead of names of persons, animals and things are called **personal pronouns**.

They are: *I, me, you, it, he, she, him, her, we, us, they, them.*

Example: The king wanted to fulfil the queen's wish. **He** grew thoughtful.

This table shows the singular and plural personal pronouns.

Singular	Plural
I, me	*we, us*
you	*you*
he, she, it, him, her	*they, them*

B. Complete these sentences with correct pronouns.

1. Rina wanted a gift from her uncle. ________ promised to buy ________ a watch soon.
2. Mr and Mrs Roy are Rahul's neighbours. ________ always helps ________ clean their garden.
3. I made sandwiches for breakfast today. Do ________ want one? ________ can eat together.
4. Sneha and her mother went to the restaurant. ________ had a pizza. ________ was delicious.
5. The teacher wanted ________ to open our English books. Then, ________ asked George to read the chapter aloud.

Study Skills

Spell Check

There are many ways of spelling the **/f/** sound in a word. You can spell it with the letter **f** (**f**lock) and with the letters **ph** (ele**ph**ant).

With the help of the clues, guess the words and spell them correctly. Each word has the /f/ sound in it.

1. The number that comes before fifteen ____________

2. We take these with a camera ____________
3. The opposite of 'male' ____________
4. It helps us to talk with someone who is far away ____________
5. It burns things ____________

Listening and Speaking

Listen to a passage about a crow and write whether these sentences are true [T] or false [F].

1. The jungle crow is brown in colour. [ ]
2. The jungle crow's call is louder than the city crow's. [ ]
3. The speaker was staying in her aunt's house. [ ]
4. Her uncle told her many stories about crows. [ ]
5. The cuckoo lays its eggs in the crow's nest. [ ]
6. The crow throws out the cuckoo chicks after they are born. [ ]

Pen it Down

21ST CENTURY Leadership

If you were the commander of the crows, how would you get food from the King of Kanchanpur's kitchen for your queen? Would you follow the commander crow's method or try a new way? What new way would you use?

Write a paragraph about it.

Self Assessment

Now I can

- read and understand a story about how loyalty is rewarded.
- complete a crossword, use binomial pairs, study collective nouns and use personal pronouns.
- spell words with the /f/ sound, and write a paragraph on a given topic.

Read More

The Monkey and the Crocodile: This *Jataka* story is about the way a clever monkey fools his false friend, a crocodile, who had wanted to kill him.

The Crow and the Snake: This story from the *Panchatantra* is about a clever crow who saves her eggs from a snake who keeps eating them up.

3

The Rooks

Jane Euphemia Browne

SUSTAINABLE DEVELOPMENT GOALS

15

Let's Get Started

The United Nations Sustainable Development Goal 15 is about life on land. It says that we must try to protect our forests and all plants, birds and animals who live on this Earth. Crows are intelligent birds which help us in many ways, They eat up tonnes of waste and thus, help to stop diseases.

Here are some interesting facts about crows. Read them and tick the ones you think are true.

1. All crows and ravens belong to the same group. ☐
2. Crows from different areas make different sounds. ☐
3. The presence of a crow has always been connected to good news. ☐
4. Some crows can understand traffic signals. ☐
5. The collective noun for a group of crows is 'murder'. ☐

HC **Happiness through Active Participation:** Participating in the collective

Reading

Have you ever seen a bird building a nest? Different types of birds use different materials to make their nests, which often vary in size and shape. Read a poem about a group of noisy rooks making their nests.

The rooks are building on the trees;
They build there every spring:
'Caw, caw,' is all they say,
For none of them can sing.
They're up before the break of day,
And up till late at night;
For they must **labour** busily
As long as it is light.

And many a **crooked** stick they bring,
And many a **slender** twig,
And many a **tuft** of **moss**, until
Their nests are round and big.
'Caw, caw.' Oh, what a noise
They make in rainy weather!
Good children always speak by turns,
But rooks all talk together.

Did You Know? Science

The rook is a bird of the crow family. It is very intelligent and can learn to make and use simple tools, such as bending a wire into a hook to pick up an object.

When do the rooks make a lot of noise?

labour: work hard

crooked: not straight

slender: thin

tuft: bunch

moss: tiny, flowerless plants that grow on damp ground

About the poet

Jane Euphemia Browne (1811–1898) was a British poet.

Comprehension

Quick Recap

A. Answer the questions in a few lines.

1. Where do the rooks build their nests?
2. In which season do they build their nests?
3. What sound do the rooks make and why?
4. How long do the rooks work?
5. Describe the rooks' nests. What are they made of?

B. Read the lines from the poem and answer the questions.

1. *They're up before the break of day, / And up till late at night;*
   a. Who does 'they' refer to?
   b. Why are they up before the break of day?
   c. Why do they work hard the whole day?

Life Skills and Values — discipline, hard work

Think and answer.

1. Are the rooks being compared to 'bad children'? Give reasons for your answer.
2. Which words do you think describe the rooks the best?
   a. noisy
   b. hardworking
   c. well-behaved
   d. early risers
   e. good singers
   f. social

21ST CENTURY Social Skills

Way with Words

ANIMAL SOUNDS

You know that rooks caw. Crows also make the same sound.

A. Match the animal with the sound it makes.

A	B
1. cat	a. hoot
2. donkey	b. croak
3. owl	c. coo
4. frog	d. hiss
5. snake	e. bray
6. sheep	f. mew
7. pigeon	g. bleat

B. Now, make sentences with any two pairs of animals and their calls.

C. Complete the sentences with the words and phrases from the poem.

1. The poor farmers have to ____________ all day in the fields to earn their bread.
2. Ahona wakes up at the ____________ ____________ ____________ to go jogging.
3. The ____________ branches of the cherry trees are heavy with fruit in spring.
4. The teacher asked the children to ____________ ____________ ____________ because she could not hear what they were saying.
5. The priest burnt a ____________ of grass while performing the ceremony.

Grammar in Use

Tenses

The **tense** of a verb tells us when an action takes place.

Examples: The rooks **make** a lot of noise. (simple present tense)
The rooks **played** with each other. (simple past tense)
The rooks **will build** their nests in spring. (simple future tense)

When the verb in a sentence tells us that the action takes place in the present time, it is in the **simple present tense**.

When the verb in a sentence tells us that the action took place in the past, it is in the **simple past tense**.

When the verb in a sentence tells us that the action will take place in the future, it is in the **simple future tense**.

A. Write the simple past tense of these verbs.

1. rise ____________ 4. try ____________ 7. know ____________
2. play ____________ 5. see ____________ 8. sing ____________
3. speak ____________ 6. pay ____________ 9. eat ____________

B. Complete the sentences with the simple future tense of the given verbs.

1. Rahel ____________ to Canada in September. (go)
2. We ____________ India's performance in the Tokyo 2020 Olympics for years to come. (remember)
3. The scientist ____________ to the lab located in the remote village. (travel)
4. When ____________ you ____________ my article on pollution? (read)
5. The artist ____________ your portrait. (draw)

C. Complete the sentences with the correct tense of the given verbs.

1. Swati __________ the story of Robin Hood tomorrow. (read)
2. Ravi __________ cheese sandwiches. (like)
3. The teacher __________ us a very interesting project to work on yesterday. (give)
4. The sun __________ in the west. (set)
5. My father __________ for a newspaper for the last five years. (work)
6. Last month, my mother __________ me a new jacket. (buy)
7. I __________ in the half marathon next month. (run)
8. Babban, the elephant, __________ in our local zoo. (live)

Study Skills

Use Your Dictionary

The words in a dictionary are always arranged in alphabetical order.

Example: If we arrange the words 'ant' and 'axe' in alphabetical order, 'ant' would come before 'axe', although both words start with the same letter, 'a'. This is because 'n' comes before 'x' in the order of letters in the English alphabet.

Circle the word in each set that is not in alphabetical order. One is done for you.

1. *near* *need* *neat* *nest*
2. catch coach coast coarse
3. train true tram trust
4. shelf shell shrill shelter
5. jacket jackal joker jolly

Listening and Speaking

A. Listen to these tongue twisters and repeat them.

1. She sells seashells on the seashore.
2. Betty bought some bitter butter.
3. Tom told Todd to eat the tasty toast.
4. The wicked witch went on her way to the west.

B. For each tongue twister, write the letter which is repeated.

Can you create a tongue twister of your own?

HC **Learning and Awareness:** New skill learning

Pen it Down

21ST CENTURY Information Literacy

Which birds do you see every day in your neighbourhood? Make a list of such birds. Then, write a short poem on one of these birds. You can write about the special feature which the bird is known for, just as rooks are known for their loud calls.

Self Assessment

Now I can

- read and understand a poem about the way rooks behave.
- match animals with their sounds, and use the simple present, past and future tenses.
- say tongue twisters aloud, and write a poem about a bird that we see every day.

Read More

The Great Brown Owl: This poem by Jane Euphemia Browne is about the owl, whose large, round eyes are open all day, but who can only see after dark.

The Grackle: This funny poem by Ogden Nash is about the grackle, a loud American bird which looks like the rook. The poet imagines him as a bully to more attractive birds.

4 Holiday Activities

Tara Goswami

Let's Get Started

Assam is famous across the world for its delicious tea. It is also known for its natural resources like oil and coal.

Complete the following passage about Assamese food and culture, using the words in the help box.

January	folk dances	seeds	three	harvest	spring	rice	lamps

The most important festival of Assam is the ______________ festival of Bihu, which is celebrated ______________ times in a year. In winter, Bhogali or Magh Bihu is celebrated in the month of ______________. Rongali or Bohag Bihu marks the beginning of the Assamese New Year during the season of ______________ in April. Kongali or Kati Bihu takes place in October. The festival is believed to protect growing crops. People usually light clay ______________ in the fields to keep away the evil eye. The traditional food prepared during all three Bihus are delicious *pithas*, which are sweet pancakes made with ______________, the most important food crop grown in Assam. *Pithas* are usually stuffed with jaggery and coconut or black sesame ______________. During Bihu, people gather in open fields and perform the Bihu dance, one of the most well-known ______________ of Northeast India.

HC **Feelings:** Contributions in relationships (siblings and grandparents)

Reading

Have you ever gone for a vacation to a place set in the middle of nature? In this story, taken from the book,* The Bogoli Phut Days, *seven-year-old Pitki talks about her experience of spending her winter holidays with her grandparents in the Sekoni Tea Estate in Assam.

Deuta went off to Calcutta the day after we reached Sekoni. I wish he had stayed. But he had some important work. We've been here for almost two weeks. It's been great fun. Dondi and I have been playing **endless** games and **exploring** the garden. The **compound** of the bungalow is huge with a sloping lawn in front where Aitama has planted lots of pretty flowers.

Why did Deuta go off to Calcutta?

endless: too many to count

exploring: moving around to find out more about something

compound: an area surrounded by a fence or a wall

organised: arranged

There is a pond with fish in it and a cowshed which has the tallest haystack nearby. Ma, Dondi and I spend lots of time on the haystack, where Ma reads to us from a book called *Watership Down*—it's about rabbits.

So we pretend to be rabbits and chew on fresh carrots from Aitama's exciting kitchen garden. The garden has all the winter vegetables. Aitama says that to be healthy, we should eat fruits and vegetables that are in season. That is the right time to eat them. Nature has made a timetable of what grows when and we should follow it.

The garden is **organised** into different plots. It has rows of peas creeping onto bamboo frames, and carrots and cauliflower and a sour, green, leafy, spinach-like vegetable called *sukaxaak*[1]. I pick these leaves and wrap them in banana leaves, and Ma helps me roast them in the fire outside where our bath water is heated. Then we invite everyone to come and eat it.

Wordwise

1. *Suka* means 'sour' in Assamese. *Sukaxaak* tastes very sour and can be eaten raw.

Did You Know? G.K.

Watership Down, by Richard Adams, is a book about the adventures of a small group of rabbits as they search for a new place to stay after their burrow is destroyed.

My favourite fruit, *bogori*[2], is in season now. It grows on the thorniest trees, but is very yummy. The fruits are sour and green when they are raw, but become red and **pulpy** as they ripen. I didn't even mind getting cuts from the thorns while trying to pick them. We always miss the *jolphai,* or olive season, but Aitama has trays and trays drying in the sun for her pickles. I've already stolen and **polished off** half the *jolphais*. They are sour and yummy too. When the pickle is ready, we can take it back home with us.

Koka got the gardener to make us two sets of bows and arrows. So Dondi and I **sling** the arrow pouches on our backs and play *shikaar-shikaar* with them. Dondi laughs at me when I shoot, but he's silly. I know I can shoot. We also have a raft or *bhur* made of banana stems in the pond and I'm almost an **expert** at rafting now. I am better than Dondi.

We went to the stream to have a mini picnic the other day. The water was cold and clear—oh, such fun! Sometimes I feel like I'm in a *Famous Five* adventure but there's just the two of us. Yesterday, Koka took us to the big stream in the middle of the forest. All of us bathed in the stream and after that we picked nice big *outenga* (elephant fruit) from under the trees. They were dropped by the elephants who love to eat this fruit. Aitama made the yummiest **tangy** dal with the fruit we picked.

Aitama doesn't let us go out in the afternoon and we have to take a nap with all the grown-ups. Aitama is very clever. She scares us by telling us about *Bura Dangoria* (the spirit of the trees) who comes and takes a nap under the trees in the afternoon. If little children come along, he catches them and takes them away! I know that there's no *Bura Dangoria* in real life, but it's good to be careful. So we stay indoors. But Aitama has to **bribe** us, so every afternoon she tells us a story. Oh, what fun it is! She tells

pulpy: soft and wet
polished off: finished eating something quickly
sling: hang
expert: very good at doing something
tangy: sour
bribe: give something valuable to someone to make them agree to do something

Which fruit did Pitki steal and eat?

Did You Know? Geography

When there are floods in Assam, people often use *bhur* or rafts to move about from place to place.

Wordwise

2. *Bogori* is an Indian fruit, known as *ber* in Hindi. There are many Assamese words in the story, like *Deuta* (father), *Aitama* (grandmother), *Koka* (grandfather) and *Bura Dangoria* (ghost).

us about kings and thieves and clever foxes and silly men and oh, so many things.

About the author

Tara Goswami is an artist, yoga teacher and writer from Shillong.

Comprehension

Quick Recap

A. Complete the sentences with information from the story.

1. Pitki's family was in Sekoni for ______________, but Deuta went off to ______________ because ______________.

2. Their mother read to the children from ______________.
3. Pitki always missed ______________. Aitama made ______________ with the fruit, which were ______________ and ______________.
4. The gardener made ______________ for the children. They also had a ______________ made of ______________.
5. Pitki sometimes felt they were in a ______________________, with just ______________.
6. Aitama told the children stories about ______________________.

B. Answer the questions.

1. How did Pitki and Dondi spend their time in Sekoni?
2. According to Aitama, why should we eat fruits and vegetables that are in season?
3. What did Pitki do with the *sukaxaak*?
4. What was Pitki's favourite fruit? Describe it. What happened when she tried to pick this fruit?
5. What were the two games that Pitki played with Dondi?
6. Where did they pick the elephant fruit? How did the fruits fall there? What did Aitama make with them?

C. Read the line from the story and answer the questions.

1. *She scares us by telling us about* Bura Dangoria...
   a. Who said these words and about whom did they say this?
   b. Who was *Bura Dangoria*?
   c. What did the speaker know about *Bura Dangoria*?

Life Skills and Values love for nature, folklore

Think and answer.

1. Do you think Pitki was afraid of *Bura Dangoria*? Why/why not?
2. Did Pitki like roaming in the woods and being in the middle of nature? How do you know?

21ST CENTURY Critical Thinking

Way with Words

Fruits and Vegetables

A. You have read about many fruits and vegetables in this story. Find seven of them in the word grid on the next page. (Tip: search from left to right and top to bottom.)

I	L	S	W	V	O	N	D	C	Z
P	U	A	S	B	L	Q	E	A	O
X	E	G	U	O	I	L	D	R	U
J	S	Z	K	G	V	Z	H	R	T
I	O	B	A	O	E	N	V	O	E
R	V	A	X	R	X	B	W	T	N
B	C	N	A	I	G	Y	H	Y	G
P	C	A	A	W	V	Y	O	E	A
I	K	N	K	E	U	K	Q	Z	F
O	F	A	Y	C	O	P	E	A	S

Contextual Usage

B. Complete the sentences with the phrases from the story.

in season | went off | spend time with | take a nap | polished off

1. I love to ______________ my cousin. She reads to me from my favourite books and plays with me.
2. When mangoes are ______________, my mother makes delicious *kheer* with them.
3. ______________ now, if you want to be awake for the cartoon show in the evening.
4. The cat ______________ the milk I gave it.
5. Sahil ______________ to school after having his breakfast of cornflakes and milk.

Grammar in Use

Prepositions of Time and Place

A **preposition** is a word that links a noun or a pronoun with other words in a sentence.

Examples: I spend lots of time **on** the haystack.
The pond has fish **in** it.

Some prepositions tell us when something happens (**at**, **on** and **in**) or about the length of time (**from**, **to**, **for**).

Examples: The library closes **at** 6 p.m.
My uncle lived in Australia **from** 2010 **to** 2020.

Some prepositions tell us where something or someone is.

Examples: on, above, over, under, below, behind, near, in front of, between

A. Complete the sentences with the correct prepositions.

1. The dog is sitting ______________ (on/under/in) the tree.
2. The bell rings ______________ (at/in/on) 12.45 p.m.
3. We walked ______________ (near/across/along) the river.
4. The horse jumped ______________ (over/on/in) the fence.
5. The boy leaned ______________ (at/on/against) the wall.
6. My mother studied in National College ______________ (from/before) 2002 ______________ 2005 (to/after).
7. The pharmacy is ______________ (in front of/before) the gate.

B. Read this passage and underline the prepositions.

Pitki and Dondi lay on the haystack and listened to a story from *Watership Down*. She thought about the day when they picked the *outenga* under the trees. She looked at the sky and saw an eagle. She dreamed of swimming in the stream near the forest.

Comparison of Adjectives

Read these sentences.

Aitama is very clever.
I am clever**er** than Aitama.
But Koka is the clever**est** of us all.
Raju is tall**er** than Meena. But Sohail is the tall**est**.

We add **-er** to an adjective when we want to compare two things or persons.

We add **-est** to an adjective when we want to compare more than two things or persons.

C. Fill in the blanks with the correct form of the given adjectives.

1. The second cake that I baked was ______________ (sweet) than the first.
2. Priya wears the ______________ (bright) colours.
3. Rohan is ______________ (young) than his brother.

4. Meeta is ________________ (clever) than Dimple.
5. The cheetah is a ________________ (fast) animal than the elephant.
6. This is the ________________ (hard) question in the test.
7. That is the ________________ (ripe) mango in the box.

Study Skills

Pronounce Well

Say the following words aloud in class. Do they end in /d/ or /t/? Write each word in the correct column. Two are done for you.

started	missed	worked	waited	needed
baked	reached	stayed	planted	polished

/d/	/t/
started	*missed*

Listening and Speaking

Listen to Neil and Ashok talk about cricket and complete the dialogue.

Neil: What is your favourite ________________?
Ashok: My favourite ________________ is cricket.
Neil: When do you ________________ ?
Ashok: I play in the ________________.
Neil: Do you bowl or do you ________________?
Ashok: I ________________ sometimes, but I mostly bat.
Neil: Which ________________ do you cheer for?
Ashok: I cheer for the ________________ team.

HC Bodily activities

Pen it Down

Complete the paragraph with the help of the given instructions.

Last year, five-year-old Neetu ____________ (*visit*, simple past) her aunt who lived ____________ (preposition) a village. ________ (pronoun) had a lot of fun there. She learned how to swim ____________ (preposition) the pond, and how to feed the cows ____________ (conjunction) buffaloes. She ____________ (*play*, simple past) ____________ (preposition) the village children too.

Self Assessment

Now I can

- read and understand a passage about holidaying in the middle of nature.
- find the names of different fruits and vegetables, learn about prepositions of time and place and understand the degrees of comparison of adjectives.
- pronounce words ending with /d/ or /t/ sounds, complete a dialogue and a paragraph.

Read More

Five Go Off in a Caravan: This book by Enid Blyton, a part of the *Famous Five* series, is about four cousins and Timmy, the dog, who solve a mystery while spending their summer holidays travelling in a caravan in England.

My Naughty Little Sister: This book by Dorothy Edwards is about a three-year-old girl who gets up to all kinds of mischief, like eating all the cake at a party!

5 The History of Chocolate

Let's Get Started

The Aztecs were a fierce tribe of warriors who ruled parts of the North American continent during the 15th and early 16th centuries.

Complete the information about the Aztecs using the help box.

exchanged	drink	Mexico	markets

The Aztecs first started making a chocolate ________.

The Aztecs ruled over ________ for over 300 years.

The Aztec calendar had only five days, with huge ________ held on every sixth day.

The Aztecs did not use money. Instead, they used the barter system, in which they ________________ necessary goods.

Learning and Awareness: Sustainable happiness

Reading

We all love to eat chocolates. But where do they come from? Do they grow on trees like fruits? Read this passage to find out how chocolate was once a drink for only kings and queens before it came to be enjoyed by ordinary people.

Chocolate comes from cocoa beans, which grow on the cacao tree. But it did not always taste the way it does today.

'A cup of chocolatl, please!'

You will be surprised to know that the first chocolate was not a solid bar. It was a **foamy** drink. It was made by the ancient Maya and Aztec **peoples** in Mexico (a country in North America) and Central America. They called it 'chocolatl' and made it from cocoa beans mixed with water. Mayans loved chocolate as much as we do today. The word 'cacao' is a Mayan word, which means 'food of the gods'.

But if you asked an ancient Mayan for a cup of chocolatl, you would not like what they would give you. Chocolatl was very bitter and not much like the hot mug of cocoa we love to drink on a winter evening.

People in Europe knew nothing about chocolate for a long time. When explorers from Spain **conquered** Central America in the sixteenth century, they brought back cocoa beans with them. But the Spanish did not want the rest of Europe to know about their discovery. So, for a hundred years, only kings, queens and nobles secretly sipped this delicious drink. However, they added sugar to make it taste nicer.

Slowly, the popularity of chocolate spread in Europe. In 1615, people drank it at a royal wedding in France. In England, in the eighteenth century, rich people visited chocolate houses—which were like today's cafes—to meet friends and have a chocolate drink.

More than two hundred years later, Daniel Peter, a famous chocolate maker in Switzerland, started adding the magic **ingredient**—**condensed** milk—to make the kind of milk chocolate that is popular today.

Around this time, a **grocer**, John Cadbury, also began to sell cocoa and drinking chocolate from his shop in England. Today, Cadbury is one of the biggest chocolate makers in the world.

Did You Know? History

The Aztecs used cocoa beans as money. An avocado cost three beans and you could buy a turkey for 100 beans! The great Aztec king, Montezuma, collected cocoa beans as taxes.

What does the word 'cacao' mean?

foamy: with small bubbles

peoples: people from different countries or regions

conquered: took over by force

ingredient: substance used to make a particular food item

condensed: made thick

grocer: a person who sells food and household items

How is chocolate made?

Starting from a cocoa bean, the process of making chocolate is a long journey. First, the cacao fruits are **harvested** by farmers in West Africa, where most of the world's chocolate is grown.

The cacao fruit, or pods, take about five months to ripen to a bright orange or red colour. Each pod, which is the size of a melon, contains about forty beans. It takes as many as a thousand beans to make just one kilogram of chocolate!

harvested: gathered crops

ground: made into a powder by crushing

What is the main ingredient of chocolate?

Cacao farmers cut the ripe pods from the trees with a sharp knife. They split open the pods with a wooden hammer and scoop out the beans with a knife. The beans are wrapped in banana leaves and dried in the hot sun. The dried beans are sold to chocolate traders, who sell them to chocolate factories across the world.

In the factories, the beans are roasted, **ground** up and melted to form 'cocoa liquor'. This is the main ingredient of chocolate.

moulds: hollow containers used to give shape to hot liquids when they cool and harden

Easter: the Christian holiday that celebrates Jesus Christ's return to life, two days after he was killed on the cross.

Then, sugar, milk and vanilla are added to the cocoa liquor. A machine stirs this chocolate mixture for a day or more. After this is done, the liquid chocolate is poured into bar-shaped **moulds** and cooled. The chocolate is ready! The solid bars are now ready to be packed and sold in the market.

Chocolate, now

Name the ingredients that are added to cocoa liquor.

Today, people all over the world eat chocolate. Many cultures have their own chocolate traditions too. For example, Christians give each other chocolate eggs to celebrate the festival of **Easter**. These are called Easter eggs. In France, people give each other chocolate fish instead of eggs.

Nowadays, many chocolate lovers buy chocolates with the 'fair trade' mark. This means that the farmers who grew the cocoa beans get paid the correct amount of money for their crops. This is a way to improve the working conditions of cacao farmers.

So, the next time you are about to bite into a piece of your favourite chocolate, remember its long journey, from a bean in a pod on a cacao tree in Africa to a bar in your hand.

Did You Know? History

The first ever chocolate bar was made in 1840 by Fry's, a British chocolate company.

Comprehension

Quick Recap

A. Read the lines from the story and answer the questions.

1. *But if you asked an ancient Mayan for a cup of chocolatl, you would not like what they would give you.*
   a. What is chocolatl?
   b. Who made it?
   c. In what way was it different from the chocolate drink we get today?

2. *Cacao farmers cut the ripe pods from the trees with a sharp knife.*
   a. What is cacao? Where does it grow?
   b. How long does it take for the pods to ripen?
   c. What do the farmers do after cutting off the cacao pods from trees?
   d. How many beans does it take to make one kilogram of chocolate?

B. Answer the questions.

1. How did chocolate reach Europe? What was the first thing added to chocolate there?
2. Who were the only people who could sip the new chocolate drink?
3. What were chocolate houses? In which country were they found?
4. What was the magic ingredient in the process of chocolate-making? Who started adding it?
5. Who was John Cadbury? Why do we know his name even today?
6. What happens to the cocoa beans in factories?
7. How do Christians use chocolate to celebrate the festival of Easter?
8. How is the Easter celebration in France different from the rest of the world?

Life Skills and Values ethical practices

Think and answer.

1. Why do you think the Spanish kept the discovery of chocolate a secret from the rest of Europe?
2. Why is the 'fair trade' mark important? Why do you think all chocolates do not have this mark?

21ST CENTURY Technology Literacy

Way with Words

SAME WORD USED AS DIFFERENT PARTS OF SPEECH

A. Choose the word that can be used to complete both the sentences in each pair.

1. Ravi and Rohan ____________ to go fishing and camping.
   Priya has a dress just ____________ mine.
   a. want b. like c. similar d. hate
2. John ____________ his mother's home at seven o'clock.
   To reach Sandy's house, take a ____________ from the market.
   a. reached b. go c. left d. right

3. The ____________ came in through the open window.
   My bag is ____________. Your bag is heavy.
   a. light   b. heavy   c. bright   d. shine

4. I ____________ a peacock yesterday.
   I want to go on the see-____________.
   a. see   b. saw   c. seen   d. met

5. ____________ your shoelaces carefully.
   The sky blue ____________ will match my white shirt.
   a. socks   b. knot   c. pants   d. tie

6. The boat will ____________ if there is a hole in the bottom.
   The plumber repaired the kitchen ____________.
   a. float   b. drown   c. sink   d. drain

B. Complete the sentences with these words and phrases from the story.

split open	scoop out	bite into	conquered	harvested	sipped

1. This sandwich looks so tasty. I can't wait to ____________ it.
2. The man ____________ his coffee slowly.
3. Soha used a spoon to ____________ the ice cream from the tub.
4. The woodman ____________ the tree trunk with his heavy axe.
5. The farmers ____________ the crop before the rains began.
6. The powerful king ____________ his neighbouring kingdom.

Grammar in Use

Question Words

We use words like **what**, **where**, **who**, **why**, **when** and **how** to ask questions.
Examples: **What** is your name?
How is chocolate made?

A. Write the questions for these answers using the given hints. One is done for you.

1. Easter eggs are gifts which people give each other during Easter. (use 'what')
   Question: What are Easter eggs?
2. It was made by the ancient Mayan and Aztec peoples. (use 'what')

3. Chocolatl was made from cocoa beans mixed with water. (use 'how')
4. In France, people give each other chocolate fish for Easter. (use 'where')
5. John Cadbury was a grocer who sold drinking chocolate in his shop. (use 'who')
6. I want to eat the cake in the evening. (use 'when' and 'you')
7. We would not like chocolatl because it was bitter. (use 'why')

CONJUNCTIONS

Conjunctions are used to join two or more words or sentences.

Look at the way conjunctions can be used to join two sentences.

Chocolate was loved by the Mayans. Chocolate was loved by the Aztecs.

Chocolate was loved by the Mayans **and** the Aztecs.

Some of the most common conjunctions are **and**, **or**, **but**, **because** and **so**.

B. Join these sentences using suitable conjunctions.

1. There is a bat under the table. There is a ball under the table.
2. I looked for my purse. I could not find it.
3. Ravi did not go to school. He was unwell.
4. Rahul likes milk. His brother likes curd.
5. Rohan asked for a banana. He was very hungry.
6. You can go to the amusement park in the evening. You can watch cartoons instead.
7. I want to learn swimming. My mother wants me to learn to play the piano.
8. Sanaya injured herself. Her mother took her to the doctor.

Study Skills

Pronounce Well

Say the words given in the box aloud. You will notice that the letter **a** is pronounced in three different ways.

Circle the words in which a is pronounced as in add.
Underline the words in which a is pronounced as in made.
Tick the words in which a is pronounced as in are.

ancient	Mayans	Daniel	father
apple	favourite	farmer	day
drank	table	started	wrapped

Listening and Speaking

Listen carefully to a short paragraph about a scary experience and answer the questions.

1. Who woke up at midnight?
2. What did she wonder about?
3. What happened to the cupboard in her room?
4. What did she place against the cupboard door?
5. Where did she run to in fear?
6. What happened in the other room?

Pen it Down

Look at the picture and write a paragraph about it.

You may think of the following questions to help you:

- What do you think the man is eating?
- What do you think has happened to the man?
- What can he use from the table to solve his problem?

Self Assessment

Now I can

- read and understand a passage on how chocolate was invented and understand the process of chocolate-making.
- use the same words as different parts of speech, use question words and join sentences using conjunctions.
- identify words with different 'a' sounds, and write a paragraph about a picture.

Read More

Charlie and the Chocolate Factory: This famous book by Roald Dahl is about a poor boy, Charlie Bucket, who wins a contest to take a tour of the mysterious chocolate factory of Willy Wonka.

The Whizz Pop Chocolate Shop: This book by Kate Saunders is about the adventures of the twins, Oz and Lily, who find out that their new house is magical, as was the chocolate their family once made.

6

The Elf and the Dormouse

Oliver Herford

Let's Get Started

Folktales are stories that have been passed down from one generation to other and were often not written down. They pass on wisdom and provide examples of common sense used to solve difficult problems.

Identify the following characters from well-known folktales using the pictures and clues.

1. 

An emperor seeks the help of his wise minister: ____________

2. 

A brave king answers questions from a ghost: ____________

3. 

A wise man solves problems with his wit: ____________

4. 

A poor boy finds a magic lamp and gets three wishes: ____________

HC **Learning and Awareness:** Clarity of purpose

Reading

Do you know what elves are? Like fairies, they are magical creatures who can fly, heal injuries and cure diseases. Turn the page and read a poem about an elf who discovered an unusual way to shelter from the rain.

Wordwise

1. A toadstool is a type of mushroom that cannot be eaten. The name came from the belief that toads often sat on these mushrooms, which look like stools.

Under a toadstool[1]
Crept a **wee** elf,
Out of the rain,
To shelter himself.

Under the toadstool
Sound asleep,
Sat a big **dormouse**
All in a **heap**.

Trembled the wee elf,
Frightened, and yet
Fearing to fly away
Lest he get wet.

To the next shelter —
Maybe a mile!
Sudden the wee elf
Smiled a wee smile,

Tugged till the toadstool
Toppled in two.
Holding it over him,
Gaily he flew.

Soon he was safe home,
Dry as could be.
Soon woke the dormouse —
'Good gracious me!'

'Where is my toadstool?'
Loud he **lamented**.
And that's how umbrellas
First were **invented**.

crept: moved with the body close to the ground

wee: tiny

dormouse: a small, mouse-like animal with a furry tail

heap: untidily piled things

trembled: shook in fear

lest: in case

tugged: pulled

toppled: fell

gaily: happily

lamented: complained

invented: created

How far away was the next shelter?

About the author

Oliver Herford (1863–1935) was an American writer and artist. He was known for his funny writings. Some of his popular poems are 'The Chimpanzee' and 'The Hen'.

Comprehension

Quick Recap

A. Answer the questions in a few lines.

1. Why did the elf come and sit under a toadstool?
2. Who was already under the toadstool? What was he doing?
3. Why was the elf frightened? Give two reasons.
4. Why did the elf smile? What did he do next?
5. According to the narrator, how were umbrellas first invented?

B. Read the lines from the poem and answer the questions.

1. *Holding it over him,/Gaily he flew.*
   a. Who is 'he' in these lines?
   b. What was he holding over himself?
   c. Where did he fly to?

2. *'Where is my toadstool?'/Loud he lamented.*
   a. Who is 'he' in these lines?
   b. What was he doing just before?
   c. Why did he lament?

Life Skills and Values common sense, humour

Think and answer.

1. Do you think the elf was clever? Give reasons for your answer.
2. Did you find the poem funny? Which lines did you find the funniest?

Way with Words

Opposite Words

A. Write the opposites of these words from the poem. Then, complete the sentences using the opposites.

1. loud - ______
2. dry - ______
3. in - ______
4. first - ______
5. wee - ______
6. gaily - ______

a. The children played in the rain and their clothes got ________.

b. The singer's voice was so ________ that no one could hear her.

c. The fairy said ________ that she could only grant the peasant one wish.

d. Rohan lives in a ________ house in the city.

e. The ________ day of school before the holidays is always the most fun.

f. The old man took ________ some coins from his pocket.

Expressions

We use certain common expressions to show feelings, such as surprise, anger, happiness and sadness.
Example: The expression, 'Good gracious me!' shows the dormouse's surprise on discovering that the elf had taken the toadstool.

B. Write the correct expressions for these sentences.

Good gracious me!	Oh no!	Ouch!	Hurrah!	Bravo!

1. ________ I pricked my finger with a pin.
2. ________ You played wonderfully in the cricket match today.
3. ________ I lost the new pen my mother gave me this morning.
4. ________ The summer holidays start from tomorrow.
5. ____________ How tall that monument is!

Grammar in Use

Common and Proper Nouns

Look at this sentence.

The elf was clever. His name was **Gem**.

In this sentence, the word **elf** is a common noun. The name **Gem** is a proper noun.

Common nouns are the names we give to all people, places, animals or things of one type.

Proper nouns are special names of people, places, animals and things.

A. Circle the proper nouns and underline the common nouns in these sentences.

1. Rahul is my brother.
2. Priya is a naughty child.
3. The Ganga is a mighty river.
4. We will visit Bangladesh in summer. My cousins live there.
5. This is my kitten. Her name is Pixie.
6. My friend, Mary went to Goa during the holidays.
7. Will you please pass me the bowl of noodles?

Inverted Commas

When someone in a story says something, we use inverted commas to mark the beginning and the end of their words.
Example: 'Where is my toadstool?' the dormouse asked.

B. Punctuate these sentences by putting inverted commas in the right places.

1. I want a glass of hot chocolate, Jaydeep said.
2. Can you get my glasses, Sana? Mother asked.
3. Good gracious me! the old woman exclaimed.
4. Ice cream! Come and have a delicious chocolate cone or a creamy vanilla cup, the ice cream vendor cried.
5. The teacher said, We are going for a picnic next week.

Study Skills

Use Your Dictionary

We use a dictionary to find the meanings of words. We can also find other information about words in a dictionary.

Look in your dictionary for the word toadstool. Tick each question whose answer you find in the dictionary.

1. How do you pronounce the word 'toadstool'? ☐
2. Where does a toadstool grow? ☐
3. Is toadstool a singular or a plural word? ☐

4. Do people eat toadstools?

5. Is toadstool a kind of mushroom?

Listening and Speaking

Imagine that you are the elf. You return home without getting wet in the rain, using the toadstool as an umbrella. Narrate your experience to your family members using these phrases:

Today, I was caught in the rain.
I was afraid that...
I noticed a...
Then I had an idea. I decided to...
Under it sat a...
That is how I...
I thought that...

Pen it Down

Look at the picture of the elf. Now, draw a picture of an elf using your own imagination and write a paragraph describing it. Try to include as many adjectives as you can think of.

Self Assessment

Now I can

- read and understand a poem about a wise elf who gets out of a difficult situation.
- practise opposites and expressions to show strong feelings.
- identify proper and common nouns and use inverted commas correctly.
- narrate an experience, and draw and describe a picture.

Read More

The Ant: This poem by Oliver Herford is about the ant that never spends its time playing, like dogs and cats do, but works hard all day.

The Elves and the Shoemaker: This well-known fairy tale by the Grimm brothers is about two elves who help a poor but kind shoemaker by making shoes for him every night.

Be Creative!

A. In the story 'A Glass of Milk', you read about people helping others in need. If you had five hundred rupees to give to an organisation which helps others, to whom would you give it? What would you want them to do with it?

Write about it in ten sentences.

B. You have learned what the Jataka tales are in 'The Faithful Act'.

Work in groups and find the names of five stories from the Jataka where an animal has helped other animals or a human being. Mention the name of the main character too.

	Name of the Jataka tale	Main character
1.	________________	________________
2.	________________	________________
3.	________________	________________
4.	________________	________________
5.	________________	________________

C. Pitki and Dondi loved to hear their mother read to them from the book *Watership Down*. Do you have a favourite writer? Have you ever wanted to write to him/her?

Write a fan letter to your favourite writer and send it to him/her using these steps:

Step 1: On a clean sheet of paper, mention the books by the writer that you have read and explain why you enjoy them. Your letter should have the date, a greeting, your name and signature.

Step 2: On another sheet of paper, draw your favourite scene from one of the writer's books. Your drawing should have the main characters from the book.

Step 3: Find the address of the writer. Sometimes you can find the address in the writer's books. Many writers have a special address for fan mail.

Step 4: Place your letter and drawing inside an envelope. Write the writer's name and the full address on it. Paste a stamp on the envelope and post it.

Note: Most writers also have an email address nowadays. Take the help of a grown-up to send your letter via email.

7

Tales from India

The Seed of Truth

Sudha Murty

Let's Get Started

Plants and trees have a lot of importance in Indian tradition. Gautam Buddha is said to have reached enlightenment under a peepal tree in Gaya, Bihar. We know this tree as the Bodhi tree today.

Think of five common plants that you see growing around you. With the help of your parents or grandparents, complete the following table about those plants. Some common plants that you could include are basil, mint, banana, eucalyptus and banyan.

Name	Local name	Uses
Sacred fig	*Peepal ka ped (Hindi)*	*relief from asthma and toothache*

HC **Active Participation:** Joy of participation in the collective

Reading

Have you ever planted a sapling and seen it grow into a plant? Read this story about Pingala, a young boy who loves gardening.

What do you think happens to the seeds he plants?

Long ago, the country of Gandhara was ruled by the just and good king, Vidyadhara. His subjects were very happy, but as the king grew older, everyone got more and more worried. The king did not have any children who could rule the kingdom after him.

The king loved gardening. He spent a lot of time taking care of his garden, planting the finest flowers, fruit trees and vegetables. One day, after he finished working in the garden, he **proclaimed,** 'I will **distribute** some seeds to all the children in the kingdom. The one who grows the biggest, healthiest plant within three months will become the prince or the princess.'

The next day there was a long line of **anxious** parents and children outside the palace. Everyone was **eager** to get a seed and grow the best plant.

Pingala, a poor farmer's son, was among these children. Like the king, he too was fond of gardening and grew beautiful plants in his backyard. He took the seed from the king and planted it in a pot with great care. Some weeks passed and he added water and **manure** to the pot, but the plant did not appear.

Pingala tried changing the soil and **transferred** the seed to another pot, but even after three months, nothing appeared.

Which country did King Vidyadhara rule?

proclaimed: said in front of everyone

distribute: give something to a number of people

anxious: worried

eager: interested and excited

manure: waste matter from animals that is used to make plants grow

transferred: (here) moved from one place to another

Did You Know? History

Gandhara was an ancient kingdom in the *Mahabharata* and the *Ramayana*. It was located in modern-day Pakistan.

Why was there a long line outside the palace?

At last, the day came when all the children had to go to the king to show the plant they had grown. They started walking to the palace, dressed in their best, holding beautiful plants in their hands.

ignoring: not paying attention to

inspection: the act of looking carefully at something

shades: colours

enveloped: (here) covered

roasted: cooked

came to the throne: became king

justly: in a fair way

What kind of seeds did the king give all the children?

Only Pingala stood sadly, watching them go by. Pingala's father had watched his son working hard with the seed and felt sorry for him. 'Why don't you go to the king with the empty pot?' he said. 'At least he will know you tried your best.'

So Pingala too wore his best dress and joined the others outside the palace, holding the empty pot in his hand and **ignoring** the laughter around him. Soon the king arrived and began his **inspection**. The pots held flowers of different **shades**, beautiful and healthy, but the king did not look happy. At the end of the line stood Pingala and when the king reached him, he stopped in surprise.

'Child, why have you come with an empty pot? Could you not grow anything?'

Pingala looked down and said, 'Forgive me, Your Highness. I tried my best, I gave it the best soil and manure I had, but the plant would not grow.'

Now the king's face broke into a smile. He **enveloped** Pingala in his arms and announced, 'Here is the crown prince! I gave everyone **roasted** seeds, which would never grow, just to see which child was the most honest and would admit he or she had not been able to grow anything. Only this boy told the truth. I am sure he will rule this kingdom one day with truth and honesty.'

And indeed that was what happened. When the king grew old and died, Pingala, who had learnt everything from him, **came to the throne** and ruled Gandhara **justly** for many years.

About the author

Sudha Murty (1950–) has written many stories for children. This story is taken from her book, *The Magic Drum and Other Favourite Stories*, a collection of folktales.

Comprehension

Quick Recap

A. Answer the questions in a few lines.

1. Who ruled the country of Gandhara?
2. Why were the people of Gandhara worried?
3. How did the king take care of his garden?
4. How did the king plan to choose the crown prince?
5. Who was Pingala? What common hobby did he share with the king?
6. What were some of the ways in which he tried to make the seed grow into a plant? Did he succeed?
7. Why did the king choose Pingala as the next ruler of the country?

B. Who said these words and to whom? Why did they say these words?

1. 'Why don't you go to the king with the empty pot?'
2. 'Could you not grow anything?'
3. 'Forgive me, Your Highness.'

Life Skills and Values

finding solutions, honesty

Think and answer.

1. Do you think the king's way of choosing the crown prince was right? Give reasons for your answer.
2. What is your opinion of Pingala based on his behaviour?

Way with Words

Proverbs

The story of Pingala is an example of the well-known proverb, 'honesty is the best policy'.

Proverbs are sayings which give advice or explain simple but deep truths about life.

A. Match the two halves of these common proverbs. One is done for you.

A	B
1. *The pen*	a. before you leap.
2. All's well	b. before they hatch.
3. Cut your coat	c. saves nine.
4. Don't count your chickens	d. that ends well.
5. Look	e. *is mightier than the sword.*
6. A stitch in time	f. is not gold.
7. All that glitters	g. according to your cloth.

B. Unjumble these words from the story. Then, use these words to fill in the blanks.

1. aegre ____________
2. nohest ____________
3. rthnoe ____________
4. eabtuiful ____________
5. fogrvie ____________
6. apearedp ____________

a. Sania never tells lies. She is an ____________ girl.

b. Ronnie loves martial arts. He is very ____________ for his karate classes to start.

c. Emperor Shah Jahan sat on the beautiful Peacock ____________.

d. The Taj Mahal is one of the most ____________ monuments in the world.

e. 'I am sorry for breaking your vase. Will you ____________ me?' the girl asked.

f. A week after Sonia planted the rose bush, a small flower ____________ on it.

Grammar in Use

Types of Sentences

Look at these sentences.

The king loved gardening.
This sentence expresses an idea or says something. It is a **statement**.

Why have you come with an empty pot?
This sentence asks something. It is a **question**.

Here is the crown prince!
This sentence shows a feeling of surprise. It is an **exclamation**. We also use such sentences to show anger, fear or admiration.

Don't let the thief run away.

In this sentence, the speaker is giving an order. It is a **command**.

Please switch off the light.

In this sentence, the speaker is asking someone for something. It is a **request**.

A. Write which types of sentences these are and make one sentence of your own of each type.

1. Please lend me your dictionary. ____________________
2. Isha's dog is very clever. ____________________
3. What a pleasant evening it is! ____________________
4. The old lady lived in a small hut. ____________________
5. Keep the bottle of juice in the fridge. ____________________
6. Where do you want to go? ____________________

Definite and Indefinite Articles

We use *a* and *an* before nouns to talk about a singular object, person or place, or when we don't refer to anything in particular. They are indefinite articles. *The* is used to talk about something particular. It is the definite article.

Examples: Pingala has **a** new plant.
The plant has beautiful flowers.

In these sentences, **a** is an indefinite article and **the** is the definite article.

B. Complete the sentences with a, an or the.

1. ________ sky is clear today. Let's go for a picnic.
2. Ravi had ________ glass of milk and ________ egg for breakfast.
3. ________ *Bible* is ________ holy book of the Christians.
4. I found ________ kitten in the drain. I took ________ kitten home because it was hurt.
5. My father is ________ pilot and my mother is ________ engineer.
6. Japan is ________ beautiful country with ________ prettiest flowers.
7. ________ javelin throw is ________ Olympic sport.
8. Rani Rampal was ________ captain of ________ Indian women's 2021 hockey Olympic team.

Study Skills

Spell Check

Homophones

There are many words which are pronounced in the same way, but are spelt differently and have different meanings. **Example:** right/write

Correct the spelling of these words so that they match the meanings of the words with the same pronunciation. One is done for you.

1. *aloud: gave permission to* ______*allowed*______
2. sail: to give something to somebody in exchange for money ____________
3. knows: the part of the face used for breathing and smelling things ____________
4. hair: an animal like a rabbit, which can run very fast ____________
5. deer: a word to describe someone whom you love very much ____________
6. peace: a part of something ____________

Listening and Speaking

21ST CENTURY Social Skills

Imagine the following situation:

Your teacher has asked you to keep the question paper for a test in the cupboard. Your best friend hears what the teacher told you and asks you to show him the paper.

What would you do in such a situation? Would you show him the question paper, or would you be honest and refuse to show it to him?

Speak on the topic in class, giving your reasons.

HC Feeling responsibility towards class and school

Pen it Down

Can you think about a time when you were honest even though it would have been easier to lie? Were you rewarded for your honesty?

Write a few paragraphs about it. Remember to explain why you were honest.

Self Assessment

Now I can

- read and understand a story about how honesty often brings us rewards.
- identify proverbs, the different types of sentences and use the definite and indefinite articles.
- spell homophones correctly, speak on a topic in class, and write a paragraph on a given topic.

Read More

The Last Laddoo: This story by Sudha Murty is about an old couple who fights over which partner should have the last laddoo.

The Cunning Fruit: This funny story by Sudha Murty narrates a man's troubles after eating a jackfruit.

8

Breakfast

Joshua Seigal

Let's Get Started

SUSTAINABLE DEVELOPMENT GOALS

3 GOOD HEALTH AND WELL-BEING

The United Nations Sustainable Development Goal 3 is about good health and well-being. It says that we should work towards the well-being of people of all ages from all parts of the world.

Read the names of the foods given in the picture and sort them into the correct columns.

Heathy Food	Junk Food

HC **Learning and Awareness:** Bodily activities and needs

Reading

What are your favourite food items? Do they include more of healthy or unhealthy

choices? Read a poem about eating a balanced meal in the morning.

What should you do when you get out of bed?

sore: painful

living dead: (here) ghost

fuel: (here) nutrition

grouchy: grumbling, complaining

slouchy: standing with shoulders and legs bent forward

shovel: push or throw large amounts of something

pouchy: (here) stomach

stuffin': (here) eating

huffin', puffin': breathing in a noisy way because you are tired

What do you do when you get out of bed
And you have a dry throat and you have a **sore** head
And you feel like one of the **living dead**?
Have breakfast.

It's a plate of **fuel** for the rest of your day
It's a bowl of power for work, rest and play
You wouldn't have it any other way –
It's breakfast.

If you don't eat it you'll feel all **grouchy**
You'll feel all shuffly, you'll feel all **slouchy**
So **shovel** it in your little **pouchy** –
Have breakfast.

It's porridge! It's toast! It's a bluberry muffin!
I'll tell you one thing and I'll tell you for nothin' —
Your belly is empty, you need to get **stuffin'**!

No more **huffin'**!
No more **puffin'**!
(Although they do eat puffin in Greenland…)
HAVE BREAKFAST!

About the poet

Joshua Seigal (1986–) is a poet and performer. He uses poetry to help children develop confidence and an interest in literature.

Did You Know? G.K.

Puffins are flightless birds which eat fish for breakfast, lunch and dinner! Their beaks change colour depending on the season.

Greenland is the world's largest island. It is located closer to Canada but is a part of the European country of Denmark.

Comprehension

Quick Recap

A. Fill in the blanks with words from the poem.

1. You have breakfast after you get out of __________.
2. Breakfast is like a plate of __________ for your body.
3. Having breakfast gives you the energy for work, __________ and __________.
4. People in __________ eat puffin.

B. Answer these questions.

1. What is the remedy for a dry throat and a sore head?
2. According to the poet, what can one have for breakfast?
3. When does one need to 'get stuffin'?

C. Read the lines from the poem and answer the questions.

If you don't eat it you'll feel all grouchy
You'll feel all shuffly, you'll feel all slouchy

1. What does 'it' refer to?
2. What should we do so that we don't feel 'slouchy'? Write the correct line from the poem and explain it in your own words.
3. At what time of the day do we have 'it'?

Life Skills and Values healthy habits

Think and answer.

According to you, which is the most important meal of the day and why?

Way with Words

Contextual Usage

A. Fill in the blanks with words from the poem.

1. Rina went to see the doctor because she has a cough and a ________________ head.
2. I have buttered ________________ and orange juice for breakfast.
3. We should eat slowly and not ________________ food into our mouth.
4. Mary bakes lovely ________________ in her little bakery.
5. ________________ is soft, thick, white breakfast dish made by boiling oats, flour or rice in milk or water.

Words Related to Taste

We use certain words to talk about taste.

Example: The blueberry muffins are **sweet** while the potato chips are **salty**.

B. Fill in the blanks with taste words from the box.

sweet	bitter	sour	mild	spicy	salty

1. The fish curry was so ________________ that it made my eyes water.
2. I don't like neem leaves because they taste ________________.
3. Tamarind is a ________________ fruit.
4. These chillies are not spicy at all. They are quite ________________.
5. The gulab jamuns my mother makes are extra ________________.
6. The vegetable stew doesn't taste good because it is too ________________.

Grammar in Use

Agreement of Subject and Verb

Look at these sentences.

Father *makes* breakfast for me.

Ritu and **Noor** *study* together.

In the first sentence, the noun **father** is singular. Hence the verb used after it, **makes**, is also singular. In the second sentence, the nouns **Ritu and Noor** are plural. Hence the verb used after them, **study**, is also plural.

This is known as the agreement of subject and verb.

A. Rewrite the sentences correctly by changing the verbs.

1. I likes to eat fish.
2. My mother cook pasta for dinner every Friday.
3. They buys vegetables from the daily market.
4. Rabab sing beautifully.
5. 'What is you eating?' asked Mother.
6. We likes to play on the beach.

Conditional Sentences

Look at the sentence.

If I could have a blueberry muffin for breakfast, I would be so happy.

The word **if** shows that the main action in the sentence can only take place if a condition is fulfilled.

I would be so happy **(main action)**

If I could have a blueberry muffin for breakfast **(condition)**

B. Match the conditions with the main actions and rewrite the sentences correctly.

A	B
1. I will take an umbrella	a. if you finish your bowl of dal.
2. The teacher will scold Hari	b. if you win the competition.
3. We will go for a picnic	c. if he reads the newspaper every day.
4. You will get a cash prize	d. if it starts raining.
5. Ravi can improve his English	e. if the weather is sunny.
6. You can have custard	f. if he doesn't complete his homework.

Study Skills

Spell Check

You will notice that words with **ee** and **ea** are often pronounced in the same way, but spelt differently.

Example: **been** and **bean**

We must be careful not to interchange **ee** with **ea** while spelling such words.

Complete these words by adding ee or ea.

1. n ____ t	3. d ____ p	5. sl ____ p	7. s ____ t	9. kn ____	11. tr ____
2. ch ____ se	4. h ____ t	6. l ____ p	8. s ____ n	10. ch ____ t	12. sh ____ t

Listening and Speaking

Look at the photograph. In pairs, describe it in your own words.

You can use the following points:

- what the boy is looking at
- the healthy/unhealthy food item in the photo
- the boy's expression

Pen it Down

21ST CENTURY Information Literacy

Work with your partner to make two lists—food items that both of you like to eat and food items that you have to eat at home as a part of a balanced diet. You should have five items in each list.

Self Assessment

Now I can

- read and understand a poem on the importance of having breakfast regularly.
- use taste words, understand the agreement of subject and verb, and practise joining sentences with 'if'.
- spell words with 'ee' and 'ea' correctly, describe a photograph and make lists of food items.

Read More

My Lunch: This is a funny poem about food by Kenn Nesbitt, in which a child puts together a lunch for himself with only his favourite sweets while his mother is asleep.

The Tummy Beast: This poem by Roald Dahl is about a greedy child telling his mother that he is always hungry because there is a person inside him who always wants delicious food.

9 Adventure at the Circus

Let's Get Started

Every year before Republic Day, the Government of India and the Indian Council for Child Welfare give National Bravery Awards to around 25 Indian children below 16 years of age for acts of bravery. This award was first given in 1957.

Read the following sentences and tick the ones which you think are acts of bravery.

1. A six-year-old girl saved her seven-year-old sister from a crocodile while they were bathing in a pond. ☐
2. Ravi helped an elderly lady carry her bag of groceries to her house. ☐
3. Asha saved two boys who were drowning without thinking about her own safety. ☐
4. Rohit saved his three-year-old brother who was trapped inside a burning house. ☐
5. Samar offered to water his neighbour's plants when she went on vacation. ☐

HC **Active Participation:** Helping others and taking responsibility

Reading

Have you been to a circus? Which was the most daring act that you saw? Read this story about a boy who saves a young girl from being hurt when an act goes wrong.

Last week, Mrs Roy made an announcement. 'Children, we will go to the circus on Wednesday. Class II will also come with us,' she said. Before she could finish, an excited buzz went up among the students of Class III.

'What fun! I want to see the clowns,' cried Neeraj, one of the naughtiest boys in the class.

Mrs Roy found it difficult to keep the class quiet, as the students whispered to each other excitedly about the trip. At lunch break, they busily discussed what they would buy at the stalls outside the circus.

Where was Mrs Roy taking the children on Wednesday?

At home, Neeraj said to his parents, 'The teacher will take us to the circus next week. Can I have some money to buy candy?'

trooped: walked together in a group

queue: line

Neeraj's parents looked at each other. They were very poor. His mother thought for a moment and replied, 'We have a week. Let me see what I can do.'

Neeraj knew how hard his mother worked. He quickly said, 'I will just take my lunch.'

Soon, Wednesday arrived. At ten o'clock, two buses with happy and excited children started from the school. They were off to the circus!

At what time did the children start from school?

At the circus grounds, the children **trooped** out of the buses and entered the tent in a **queue.**

In the first act, a group of clowns walked in, wearing funny hats and bright costumes. They juggled balls, chased one another and fell down in their hurry. How the children laughed!

Who made the children hold their breaths with their moves?

Did You Know? G.K.

The Well of Death is a show in which vehicles go round and round in a big well-shaped stage, while the audience watches from the top. It is less common these days as drivers can be seriously injured during the act.

Then came the acrobats, riding tall **unicycles**, and **trapeze artists** who made the children hold their breaths with their moves.

'I can do all that,' Neeraj **boasted** to his friend Ravi.

'Don't you show off! You fell off your bicycle last week when you tried to prove that you could ride without using your hands,' Ravi laughed.

The next act was the Well of Death. A man rode a motorcycle along the wall of a tall **arena** built like a cylinder. Round and round he went, and rode up to the very top. The children were amazed. They clapped again and again.

But suddenly, something went wrong. The children saw the man come riding out of the cylinder and into the area where they sat. 'His tyre has burst!' someone shouted.

The motorcycle rushed along the path between the chairs at great speed, while the rider tried to stop it. Everyone **scrambled away**, but a little girl, who had been too slow to get up, stood fixed to the spot, too scared to move.

unicycles: cycles with one wheel

trapeze artist: someone who performs with a wooden bar hanging from two pieces of rope high above the ground

boasted: spoke too proudly

arena: an open area with seats around it

scrambled away: moved out quickly

But Neeraj had seen her. She was little Neha from the second standard, who had been sitting two rows behind him. He was beside her in a flash and pulled her out of the way moments before the motorcycle rushed past.

The motorcycle came to a stop and the rider got off. He rushed to Neha. The owner of the circus and Mrs Roy came running too.

'Are you alright?' the rider asked.

'Yes,' Neha replied in a small voice. '*Bhaiyya* saved me.'

'You were really brave,' Ravi whispered to Neeraj.

Everyone went back to their seats. The circus started again. Neha sat beside Neeraj for the rest of the show.

Afterwards, the children crowded around the food stalls. Neeraj had no money. He stood quietly in a corner.

Neha's parents had come to take her home and heard of Neeraj's bravery. They came up to him and hugged him. 'Thank you for saving our daughter,' Neha's mother said, touching his head.

Together they went to the food stall, where Neeraj had his favourite banana chips.

As he sank his teeth into a chip with a **satisfying** crunch, he thought, 'It's a good day.'

Did You Know? **History**

The first modern circus was set up almost 300 years ago by Philip Astley, an English army officer, to show horse riding tricks in London.

What did Neeraj have at the food stall?

satisfying: something which makes you happy

When Neeraj came home in the evening, his mother asked, 'Did you enjoy the circus? Which act did you like the best?'

There was a big smile on Neeraj's face as he told her what had happened at the circus.

'You were very brave, my son,' his mother said after he finished his story.

'It was the best day of my life!' Neeraj exclaimed.

Comprehension

Quick Recap

A. Number the sentences in the order of the events in the story.

1. Mrs Roy took the students to the circus on Wednesday. ☐

2. Acrobats rode tall unicycles and trapeze artists performed daring acts.

3. The students discussed what they would buy from the food stalls.

4. The man rode his motorcycle into the area where the children sat.

5. Neha's parents bought Neeraj banana chips.

6. Neeraj pulled Neha out of the motorcycle's way.

B. Answer the questions.

1. Why did Mrs Roy find it difficult to keep the class quiet?
2. Which were the two classes taken to the circus? Which class did Neeraj study in?
3. What did the children see in the first act?
4. What was the Well of Death? What went wrong with it?
5. Who was Neha? How did Neeraj help her?
6. What did Neha's parents do when they met Neeraj?

C. Read the line from the story and answer the questions.

1. *'Don't you show off!'*
   a. Who said these words and to whom?
   b. When did he say these words?
   c. What did the speaker say next?

Life Skills and Values

selflessness, kindness

Think and answer.

1. Was Neeraj a good son? Give reasons for your answer.
2. Neeraj went to Neha's rescue even though everyone else rushed to save themselves. What does Neeraj's action tell you about him?
3. Do you think we should watch dangerous acts like the Well of Death? Why/Why not?

Way with Words

Sound Words

Look at these sentences.

An excited **buzz** went up among the students.

He sank his teeth into a chip with a satisfying **crunch**.

The words **buzz** and **crunch** are similar to the actual sounds they refer to. They are sound words.

A. Complete the sentences with these sound words.

splash	rattled	zoomed	hissed	screeched	neighed

1. Neeraj jumped into the swimming pool with a big ________.
2. The race car ________ past me.
3. The snake ________ when it was disturbed.
4. The van ________ to a halt to avoid hitting the dog.
5. The horse ________ loudly when it saw the jockey.
6. The windows ________ in the storm.

Movement Verbs

Look at these sentences.

Everyone **scrambled** away.

The children **trooped** out of the buses.

The verbs **scrambled** and **trooped** describe movement.

B. Match the movement verbs with their meanings and make sentences with them.

movement verb	meaning
1. march	a. pull something along with difficulty
2. leap	b. move forward on one's hands and knees
3. drag	c. jump into the water
4. crawl	d. walk with regular steps like a soldier
5. dive	e. jump

Grammar in Use

Adverbs

Look at this sentence.

The students whispered to each other **excitedly**.

The word **excitedly** describes the verb 'whispered'. It tells us *how* the students whispered. It is an adverb.

Words that describe verbs are known as **adverbs**.

A. Underline the verbs that the adverbs in bold describe.

1. He walked into the room **silently**.
2. Sumit was whistling **merrily** as he walked down the road.
3. The sun shone **brightly** through the clouds.
4. He sat **comfortably** on the sofa.
5. He replied **rudely** to her question.

Two common ways of forming adverbs from adjectives are by:

- adding **-ly** after the adjective.
  Example: loud → loud**ly**
- changing the **y** to **i** and adding **-ly** after the adjective when it ends with **y**.
  Example: happy → happ**ily**

B. Make adverbs from the adjectives given in the box. Then, use the adverbs to complete the sentences.

quick	careful	hungry	excited	beautiful	quiet	easy	angry

1. The old man crossed the busy road __________.
2. Ram lifted the heavy suitcase __________.
3. Rina always walks very __________.
4. Priya sings and dances __________.
5. The teacher is absent but the class is sitting __________.
6. The thin cat __________ drank the milk which Azeem gave her.
7. Ravi was talking __________ with his friends.
8. The lion roared __________.

Study Skills

Pronounce Well

Say the following words ending with **-ure** aloud. You will notice that they are pronounced in two different ways. Some rhyme with the word 'treasure' while the others rhyme with the word 'cure'.

Now, circle the words that rhyme with treasure. Underline the words that rhyme with cure.

sure	capture	leisure	pleasure	pure
mixture	nature	adventure	measure	creature

Listening and Speaking

Listen to three conversations about people asking for permission. Then, in pairs, have conversations asking for permission to do the following:

- to visit a friend's house to play (ask your parents)
- to go to the library (ask your teacher)
- to use someone's pen

Pen it Down

21ST CENTURY Media Literacy

Create a poster for a travelling puppet show.

You should include the following information:

- name of the puppet show
- dates and venue
- the stories or folktales that will be enacted
- the names of the puppeteers or artists, and other highlights

Self Assessment

Now I can

- read and understand a story about people risking their own lives to save others.
- use sound words and movement verbs, and make adverbs from adjectives.
- pronounce words ending with *-ure*, ask for permission and create a poster.

Read More

Mr Galliano's Circus: This book by Enid Blyton narrates the adventures of Jimmy Brown when Mr Galliano's Circus comes to their town.

Kali and the Rat Snake: This story by Zai Whitaker is about Kali, the son of a snake catcher. He becomes a hero after catching a rat snake which had sneaked into his classroom.

10

Two Little Kittens

Let's Get Started

Pets are great companions and offer us a lot of love and comfort. It is important to take care of them and make sure that they are safe.

Look at the poster and create a list of what pet owners should do and what they should avoid. Use the poster as a guide.

HC **Learning and Awareness:** Harmony in relationships

Reading

Have you seen cats fight with each other? How do they behave? What kind of sounds do they make? Read a poem about two kittens fighting on a stormy night.

Two little kittens, one stormy night,
Began to **quarrel**, and then to fight;
One had a mouse, the other had none,
And that's the way the quarrel began.

'I'll have that mouse,' said the biggest cat;
'You'll have that mouse? We'll see about that!'
'I will have that mouse,' said the eldest son;
'You shan't have the mouse,' said the little one.

I told you before 'twas a stormy night
When these two little kittens began to fight;
The old woman **seized** her sweeping broom,
And **swept** the two kittens right out of the room.

The ground was covered with **frost** and snow,
And the two little kittens had nowhere to go;
So they laid them down on the mat at the door,
While the old woman finished sweeping the floor.

What did the biggest cat want?

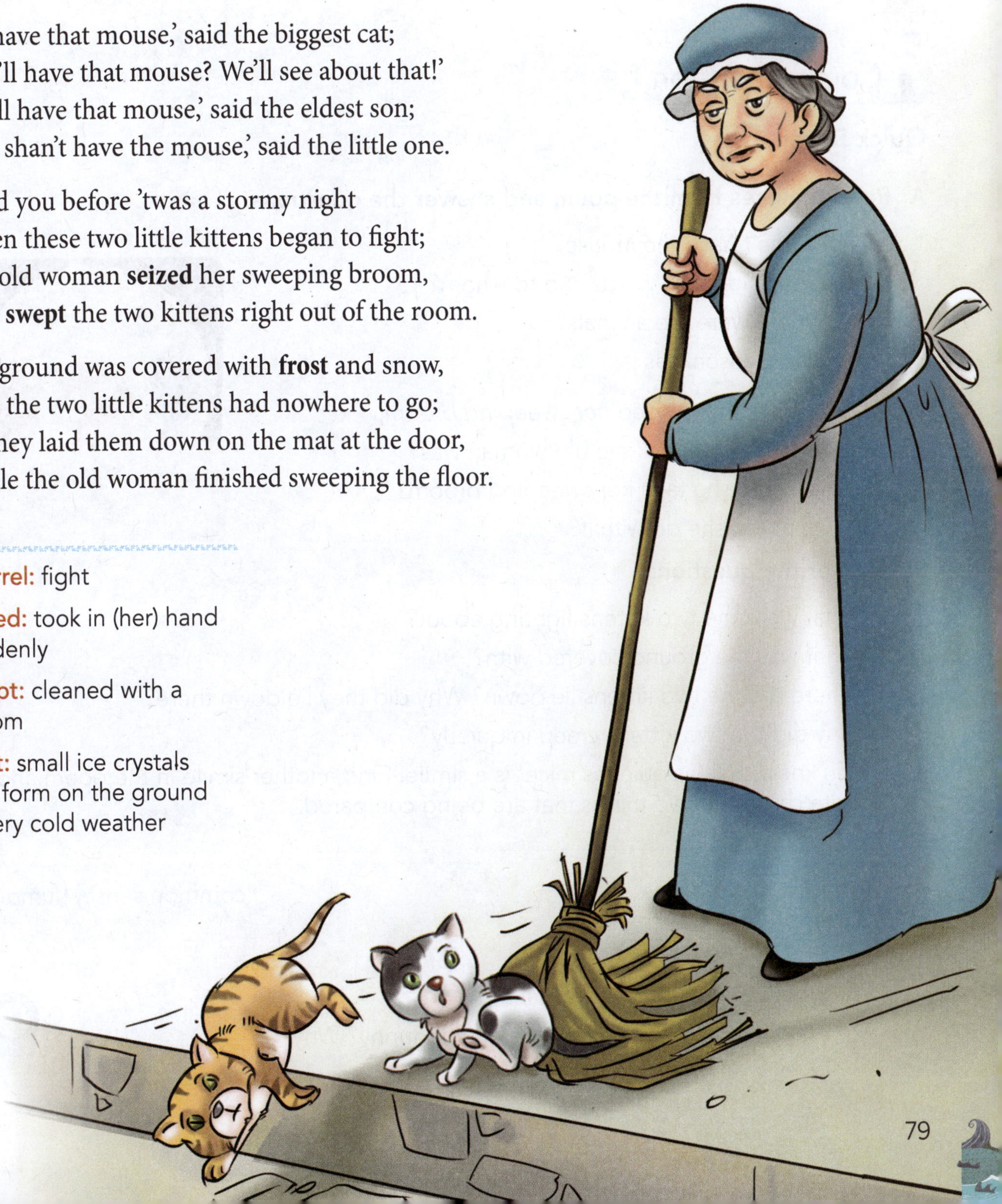

quarrel: fight

seized: took in (her) hand suddenly

swept: cleaned with a broom

frost: small ice crystals that form on the ground in very cold weather

Then they **crept** in, as quiet as mice[1],
All wet with the snow, and cold as ice,
For they found it was better, that stormy night,
To lie down and sleep than to quarrel and fight.

Literary term

1. This is a **simile**. The poet compares the kittens to mice, which move so quietly that no one notices them.

crept: moved slowly

Comprehension

Quick Recap

A. Read the lines from the poem and answer the questions.

1. *'You shan't have the mouse,'*
   a. Who said these words and to whom?
   b. Where were the animals?
   c. What season was it?
2. *The old woman seized her sweeping broom,*
   a. Who do you think the old woman was?
   b. Why did she take her sweeping broom?
   c. What did she do with it?

B. Answer the questions.

1. What were the two kittens fighting about?
2. What was the ground covered with?
3. Where did the two kittens lie down? Why did they lie down there?
4. Why did the two kittens creep in quietly?
5. You know that 'as quiet as mice' is a simile. Find another simile in the poem and write down the two things that are being compared.

Life Skills and Values — common sense, humour

Think and answer.

1. What lesson did the kittens learn?
2. Which parts of the poem did you find funny? Why?

21st Century Critical Thinking

Way with Words

PREFIXES

We can form new words by adding letters to them. **Example:** covered → **un**covered

A. Add un, dis or in to make new words. One is done for you.

1. __in__ door
2. ____ appear
3. ____ happy
4. ____ pack
5. ____ complete
6. ____ lucky
7. ____ agree
8. ____ correct
9. ____ tidy

B. Write the words related to the winter season from the poem.

C. Write down the words from the poem which match these descriptions.

1. what you do at the end of the day after closing your eyes: __________
2. a small, furry animal which cats love to chase: __________
3. something with which you clean the floor: __________
4. a house is divided into these: __________
5. what you become if someone pours water on you: __________
6. when there is thunder, and strong winds blow: __________

Grammar in Use

CONTRACTIONS

Look at the sentence.

'I'll have that mouse,' said the biggest cat.

In the above sentence, the words **I will** have been shortened to **I'll**. In the shortened word, the letters **wi-** have been replaced with an apostrophe (').

Now, look at a few more sentences in which the verb has been shortened.

It's as cold as ice. (It is)

You'll have that mouse? (You will)

She's the lady of the house. (She is)

Here's the sweeping broom. (Here is)

A. Shorten the underlined words and rewrite the sentences.

1. There is an aquarium in the hotel lobby.
2. I am going to the zoo on Sunday.
3. It is a beautiful morning.
4. Let us help Rahul with his project.
5. We will complete the holiday homework today.
6. We are going to the park.

Negative Sentences with Not

We can change a sentence to its negative form by adding **not**.

Examples: She seized her broom. → She did **not** seize her broom.
The cats were feeling cold. → The cats were **not** feeling cold.

B. Add not to make negative sentences. You may have to change the form of the verb in some sentences.

1. My aunt is a teacher.
2. I have completed the housework.
3. I returned the library book on time.
4. Mala enjoys writing poetry.
5. Mrs Roy waited for her son to return home.
6. I want to be a scientist when I grow up.

Study Skills

Use Your Dictionary

Many words have more than one meaning, even though they are spelt in the same way.

Look in your dictionary and write as many meanings of these words as you can find.

1. mouse ____________________

2. old ____________________

3. lie ____________________

4. right ____________________

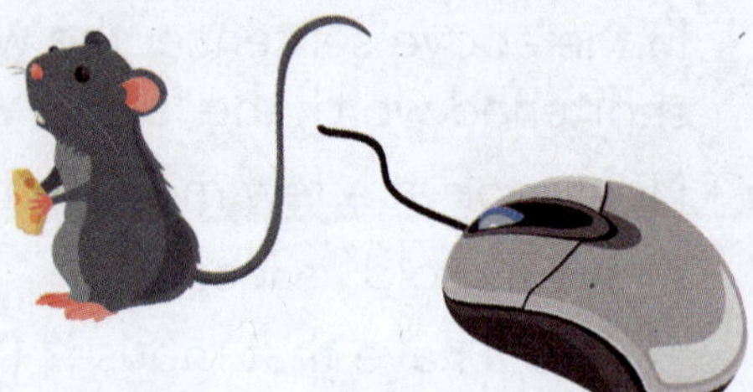

Listening and Speaking

Do you sometimes argue over small things with friends?
Listen to two students arguing about a book.

In pairs, think of a topic about which you recently disagreed with a friend. Act out the situation after writing out the dialogue that each of you will say. You should show how you solved the disagreement in a friendly way.

You can include these lines:

I will have/do...
You won't have/do...
We'll see about that!

Pen it Down

You had a fight with your best friend. Write a letter to him/her saying you are sorry for your rude behaviour.

You should mention the following points in your letter:

- the reason for your behaviour
- your wish to be friends again
- a promise to be careful about your friend's feelings in future

Self Assessment

Now I can

- read and understand a poem about solving problems in a friendly way rather than fighting.
- learn to use prefixes, the shortened forms of words and make negative sentences using *not*.
- enact a given situation and write a letter to a friend.

Read More

A Kitten: This poem by Eleanor Farjeon is about a curious kitten who plays around the house continuously until it goes off to sleep.

Koko's Kitten: This true story by Dr Francine Patterson is about the friendship between Koko, a gorilla who speaks sign language, and a kitten.

11

Anna's Experiments with Weather

Nandita Jayaraj
Priya Kuriyan

Let's Get Started

Read these facts about one of the most famous women scientists in history, Marie Curie, and complete the graphic organiser. Use the words from the help box.

governess | University | World War | twice | polonium, radium

She discovered two new metals, ______ and ______

She was the first and only woman to win the Nobel Prize ______.

She made X-ray machines that could be moved to hospitals during ______ ______ I.

She worked as a ______ to support her higher education.

She went to the secret Flying ______ which allowed women to study.

Learning and Awareness: Exploring the meaning of education

Reading

There are many remarkable women in the history of India who made the country proud in various fields of science and the arts. This story graphic is about one such extraordinary

woman. Read about a little girl from Kerala who went on to become one of India's greatest weather scientists.

peered: looked

sparkling: shining brightly

Encyclopaedia: a series of books about facts, arranged in alphabetical order

hugging: putting one's arms around a person one likes

Anna loved to read books on science the most. She also read about Mahatma Gandhi and Vaikom Satyagraha. She became a **devoted** follower and started wearing **khadi** clothes.

After school, she went on to study **physics** and **chemistry** at Pachaiyappa's College in Chennai.

In 1940, many years and many, many books later, Anna got a scholarship to work in the **laboratory** of the famous Nobel Prize-winning scientist C. V. Raman in Bengaluru.

The scientist pointed to a box. What was inside the box?

But this time, the diamonds were not for wearing. They were for experiments. Dr Raman wanted Anna to find out what makes diamonds shine. So, she read books about diamonds. Books, books and more books!

Being a scientist was the best! Anna could study anything she wanted. She did like things that shine. And what shines brighter than diamonds?

Anna wanted to read books about the sun, sunlight and weather.

Did You Know? History

Vaikom Satyagraha was a movement against caste inequality that began in Travancore. Mahatma Gandhi came there to support the movement in 1921.

devoted: loyal

khadi: cloth made by hand in India from a natural material, such as cotton

physics, chemistry: special areas of science, taught as separate subjects

laboratory: a place where experiments are done

So, in 1945, she left for England to study **meteorology** at the Imperial College, London.

Books, books and more books!

Anna did hundreds of experiments and read many more books.

In 1948, she returned to India and joined the Indian Meteorological Department in Pune. She published many **research** papers on meteorological instruments.

She built many gadgets or machines to measure the weather of a place.
'How sunny is it in Mumbai?'
Anna built a gadget to measure that.
'How windy is it in Chennai?'
Anna built a gadget for that too.

In 1962, she started work on her pet project. It was a special balloon called ozonesonde. It had a small machine fixed to it. The machine measured a gas found in the air called **ozone**.

Look, there goes Anna's ozonesonde!

meteorology: the scientific study of the Earth's atmosphere and weather conditions
research: studying something to discover new information about it
ozone: a colourless gas that protects the Earth's atmosphere

In 1976, Anna Mani retired as the Deputy Director General of the India Meteorological Department.

She never got married. She **dedicated** her life to her studies and hobbies. She loved **trekking** and bird watching, and became a member of many scientic organizations, such as the Indian National Science Academy. And in all this time, she continued to make gadgets.

She became one of the wisest weather scientists in India.

Even as she grew older and more well-known, her best friends remained the same.
Books, books and more books!

In the 1980s, she even started her own company to make gadgets.

In her factory she could build anything! She built nearly a 100 weather gadgets in her lifetime.

Sadly, a stroke in 1994 left her unable to move. On 16 August 2001, Anna Mani quietly passed away in Kerala.

Her work showed the way for other scientists, especially women scientists, who came after her. Anna Mani's life shows us that it is possible to be anything, if you set your mind to it.

dedicated: spent a lot of time doing something

trekking: making a long journey on foot to enjoy nature

Comprehension

Quick Recap

A. Underline the correct word or phrase to complete each sentence.

1. She got a watch/a dress/diamond earrings on her birthday.
2. After reading about Mahatma Gandhi and the Vaikom Satyagraha, Anna began to wear khadi/silk/woollen clothes.
3. The diamonds in the laboratory were meant to be worn/used in experiments/gifted.
4. Anna built many gadgets to measure the climate/length/height of a place.
5. Her favourite gadget was a special car/robot/balloon.

B. Answer these questions.

1. Why was Anna disappointed with her birthday gift?
2. What did Anna study after school and where?
3. What did the scientist want Anna to do with the diamonds?
4. What were Anna's hobbies?

C. Read the line from the story and answer the questions.

1. *Being a scientist was the best!*
   a. Who is being referred to as a scientist?
   b. Why did the person referred to enjoy being a scientist?
   c. Where did this person go to in 1945 and why?

Life Skills and Values — curiosity, education

Think and answer.

1. Do you think Anna Mani was different from most other women, especially in her time? Why/why not?
2. Which quality of Anna Mani did you like the most? Give reasons for your answer.

Way with Words

Words Related to Science

There are many words related to science in the story. How many can you remember?

A. Read the clues and complete this crossword puzzle.

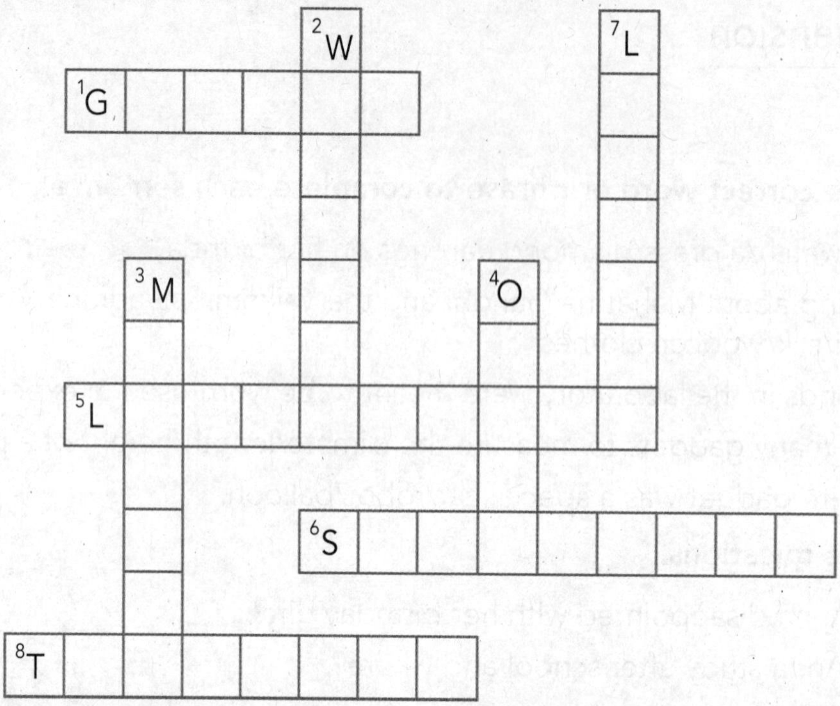

Across

1. a mechanical or an electronic device (6)
5. a place where experiments are conducted (10)
6. a person who studies natural or physical sciences (11)
8. mountain climbing as a hobby (8)

Down

2. We describe this as cold, sunny, windy, rainy, etc. (7)
3. to find the amount or size of something (7)
4. a type of gas found in the air (5)
7. a place to read, which has a lot of books and magazines (7)

HOMOPHONES

Read these sentences.

Anna's gadget **flew** high in the sky.

She sneezed loudly because she had the **flu**.

The words **flew** and **flu** have the same pronunciation but different meanings. They are **homophones**.

B. Tick the correct word from the homophones in these sentences.

1. I went to meet/meat my friend yesterday.
2. The bear/bare climbed the tree to get some honey.
3. My mother gave me some money for my bus fare/fair.
4. Please iron my blew/blue shirt.
5. The teacher asked the children not to brake/break the toys.

C. Make sentences with the homophones of the underlined words.

1. Do you know what Anna really wished for?

   ____

2. The diamonds were for experiments.

   ____

3. 'Happy Birthday, dear Anna.'

   ____

4. Anna Mani blew out all eight candles.

   ____

5. She had only one small wish.

   ____

Grammar in Use

Subject and Predicate

We can divide a sentence into two parts: a subject and a predicate.

Look at the sentence.

Anna loves reading books.

Here, **Anna** is the subject and **loves reading books** is the predicate.

The **subject** of a sentence is the person or thing that the sentence is about.

The **predicate** is what the sentence says about the person or thing.

Remember, the predicate always includes the verb.

A. Complete the sentences by adding suitable subjects or predicates. One has been done for you.

1. *The naughty children plucked mangoes from the tree.*
2. ______________________ was kept on the desk.
3. ______________________ was blowing the whistle.
4. The newspaper ______________________.
5. I ______________________.
6. Rashi's birthday cake ______________________.
7. The cricketer ______________________.
8. ______________________ saw a herd of deer.

Pronouns

Read these sentences.

The weather gadgets were **hers**.

'All the books in the library are **yours**, Anna!'

This is Anna's own factory.

The highlighted words **hers**, **yours** and **this** are pronouns.

Pronouns such as *mine*, *yours*, *his*, *hers* and *theirs* show that something belongs to someone. These are called **possessive pronouns**.

Pronouns such as *this*, *that*, *these* and *those* that point to something or someone are called **demonstrative pronouns**.

B. Complete the sentences with the correct set of pronouns from the box.

that, theirs	this, ours	that, yours	this, mine	that, his	these, those

1. ____________ is my book. It is ____________.
2. ____________ is their car. It is ____________.
3. ____________ are your keys. ____________ are mine.
4. ____________ is your room. That is ____________.
5. Is ____________ the desk which belongs to us? Yes, it is ____________.
6. ____________ is Jason's coat. It is ____________.

Study Skills

Pronounce Well

Say the words in the box aloud. Do they begin with a sh or a s sound? Now write the words in the correct column. Two are done for you.

shower	social	shirt	shine	sun	sniff	snow
shame	soak	sure	sail	shouted	summer	sugar

sh sound	s sound
shower	*social*

Listening and Speaking

Listen carefully to the passage and answer the following questions

1. What was Anna's full name?
2. Which language did she speak at home?
3. What is the current name of the Indian state in which she was born?
4. What advice did Anna get and from whom?
5. When and why did Anna go to Egypt?
6. What did Vikram Sarabhai ask Anna to do?

Pen it Down

21ST CENTURY Creativity

Write a poem in eight lines about women who want to study science.

The following points can be included in your poem:

- importance of science in our lives
- fun with experiments
- names of some women in science like Anna Mani and Kalpana Chawla
- use of rhyming words like *treasure-measure*, *mass-pass*, *books-looks*

Self Assessment

Now I can

- read and understand a graphic story about one of India's early weather scientists.
- complete a crossword on words related to science, and practise homophones.
- understand subject and predicate, and possessive and demonstrative pronouns.
- identify words with *sh* or *s* sounds, and write a poem.

Read More

Little People, Big Dreams – Marie Curie: This graphic story by Maria Isabel Sanchez Vegara and Frau Isa tells us about the famous scientist Marie who couldn't go to college because she was a woman. However, she went on to win the Nobel Prize for Physics due to her discoveries that helped in the fight against cancer.

31 Fantastic Adventures in Science – Women Scientists in India: This book by Aashima Dogra and Nandita Jayaraj includes stories of women scientists from India who overcame difficult circumstances to succeed.

12

Kangaroos

John Cotton

Let's Get Started

Learn more about these creatures from Australia. Identify and write their names using the given clues.

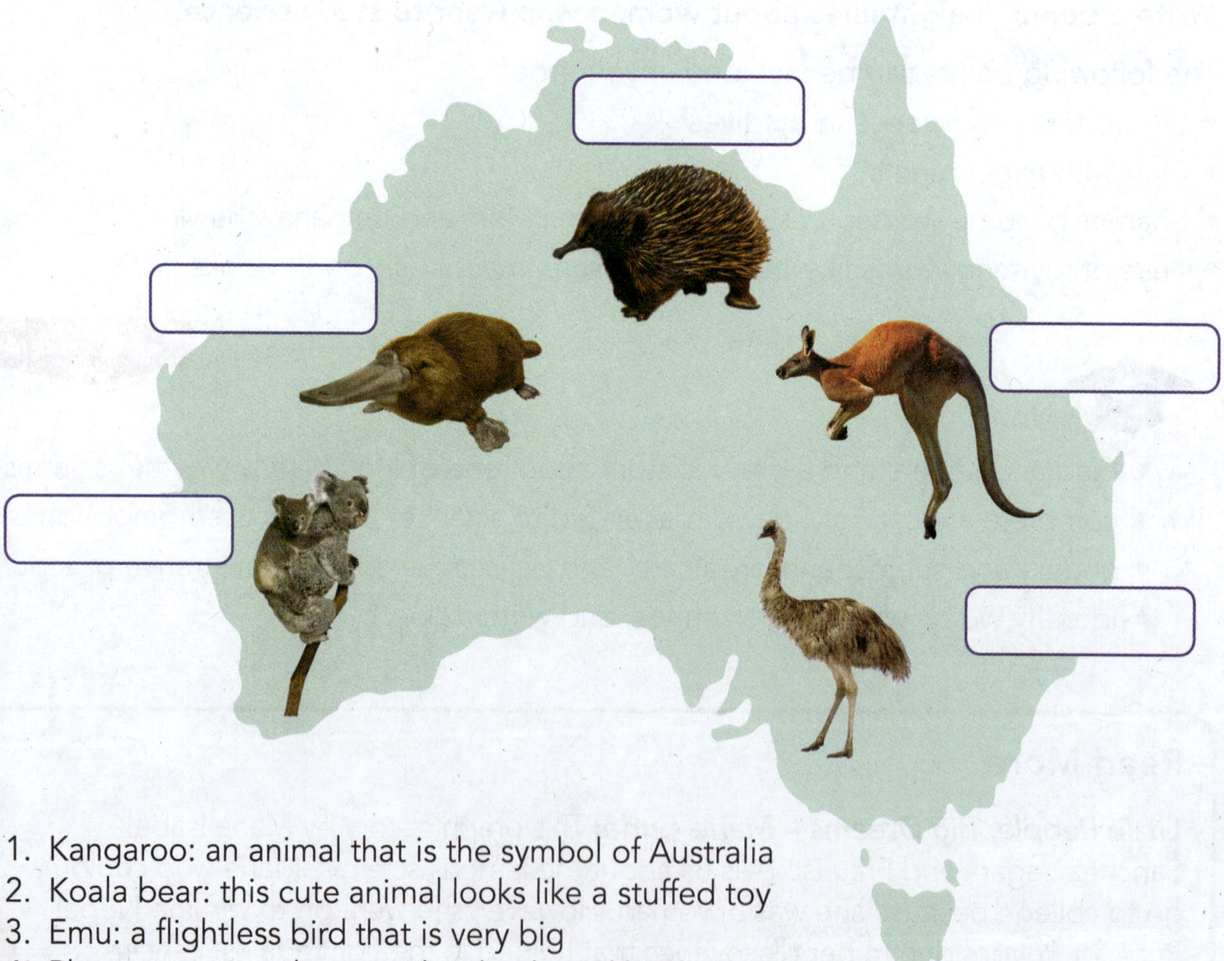

1. Kangaroo: an animal that is the symbol of Australia
2. Koala bear: this cute animal looks like a stuffed toy
3. Emu: a flightless bird that is very big
4. Platypus: a very shy animal with a broad beak
5. Spiny anteater: this tiny animal catches and eats ants using its long, sticky tongue

Active Participation: Recognizing characteristics and intrinsic nature of entities

Reading

Kangaroos are marsupials found in Australia. They carry their babies in a pouch or pocket in their bodies. They cover huge distances with a giant leap. Read this fun poem about the world's largest marsupial.

Kangaroos[1] are hoppity
Kangaroos are fun,
If you want to catch a kangaroo
You'll really have to run.

Kangaroos are jumpy
Bounding over the plain,
You can't **hold down** a kangaroo
'Cause he'll bounce up again!

Kangaroos are **tough** guys
They can box as well,
If a kangaroo should hit you
Your head rings like a bell!

Kangaroo mums are kindly
For their young they have a pocket,
Where babies can feed and feel quite safe
While mum takes off like a rocket!

bounding: running with long steps

hold down: to stop someone from moving

tough: strong

What do kangaroo babies do in a pocket?

Wordwise

1. The kangaroo's name comes from an Australian tribal language, in which it is called *gangurru*.

About the poet

John Cotton (1925–2003) was a British poet and a teacher. He wrote many collections of poetry, such as *Oh Those Happy Feet* and *Here's Looking at You, Kid.*

Comprehension

Quick Recap

A. Complete the sentences with words and phrases from the poem.

1. You have to run very fast to ______________________.
2. Kangaroos like to go running over ______________________.
3. If you try to hold down a kangaroo, it will ______________________.
4. Kangaroo mums keep their babies ______________________.

B. Read the lines from the poem and answer the questions.

1. *Kangaroos are tough guys*
   a. What does the phrase, 'tough guys' mean?
   b. What can kangaroos do that show that they are tough?
   c. What would happen if a kangaroo hits someone?
2. *Where babies can feed and feel quite safe*
   While mum takes off like a rocket!
   a. Who is the poet talking about in these lines?
   b. Where do the babies feel safe?
   c. What does the phrase 'take off like a rocket' mean?

Life Skills and Values nature, animals

Think and answer.

1. List the words from the poem which show that kangaroos are very energetic and active animals.

21ST CENTURY Information Literacy

Way with Words

A. Complete the sentences with words from the poem.

1. The boys looked across the ______________ but could not find the missing cattle.
2. Put the coins in your ______________.
3. The dog went ______________ over the playground.
4. The ______________ exploded as it landed on the ground.
5. Tom can ______________ a basketball fifteen times in a row.

RHYMING WORDS

B. Find two words from the poem which rhyme with each of these words. To each set, add a rhyming word of your own.

1. bun __________ __________ __________
2. main __________ __________ __________
3. fell __________ __________ __________
4. locket __________ __________ __________

Grammar in Use

SUBJECT, VERB AND OBJECT

Look at this sentence.

Kangaroos eat **grass**.

You know how to find the subject and the verb in a sentence. Here, **kangaroos** is the subject, while **eat** is the verb.

To find the object in a sentence, we add the questions *who* or *what* after the verb.

Question: Kangaroos eat *what*?

Answer: Kangaroos eat grass.

So, **grass** is the object of the verb **eat** in the sentence.

A. Circle the subjects, underline the verbs and tick the objects in these sentences.

1. The king loved his faithful horse.
2. Hiya dislikes horror films.
3. Joy met Deepak in the park.
4. Tintin plays the piano every day.
5. I like painting.
6. My brother plays cricket for his school team.

NEGATIVE CONTRACTIONS

Look at the sentence.

You **can't** hold down a kangaroo.

Here, the word **cannot** has been shortened to **can't** by replacing the letters **-no-** with an apostrophe.

We follow the same rule to shorten certain verbs followed by **not**.

Examples: does not → **doesn't** should not → **shouldn't**

B. Complete the sentences with the correct negative contractions from the box.

doesn't	couldn't	wasn't	isn't	won't	can't

1. I ______________ go for the concert tonight because I am not well.
2. Don't ask Raman to go to the market. He ______________ know the way.
3. The naughty child ______________ write neatly.
4. Ravi ______________ watch the match because he fell asleep.
5. ______________ Sheela your cousin?
6. There ______________ any water in the house yesterday.

Study Skills

Spell Check

The word **kangaroo** has the same two letters, **-oo** in the end.

Complete the names of these animals by adding the same two missing letters.

1. bab _ _ n	4. squi _ _ el	7. bu _ _ alo
2. ch _ _ tah	5. gira _ _ e	8. g _ _ se
3. a _ _ igator	6. d _ _ r	9. ra _ _ it

Listening and Speaking

In pairs, play a game where you describe an object and your partner identifies it. Take turns to describe the object and guess the answer.

Use the following steps:

- Think of an object. It should be something which you have read about in the previous chapters. **Examples:** chocolate, haystack, kitten, broom
- Use five sentences to describe it. You can talk about the way it looks, where it is found, what it is used for and what it tastes like.
- You get points depending on how many questions each of you takes to guess the right answer. The fewer the questions, the higher the score.
- Play five rounds of the game. The person with the highest score wins!

Pen it Down

A. Imagine that you are a baby kangaroo, looking at the outside world from your mummy's pocket. Write five sentences about what you see.

B. Paste a picture of a kangaroo in your notebook. Write the name of the country where it is found. Write five sentences about the kangaroo using the facts that you can find in your school library or on the Internet.

HC Recognizing characteristics and intrinsic nature of entities

Self Assessment

Now I can

- read and enjoy a poem about kangaroos, who can be energetic and playful animals.
- identify rhyming words, find the subject, verb and object in a sentence, and use negative contractions.
- use double-letter words, play a describing game, and write sentences on a given topic.

Read More

My Cat Goes Flying Through the Air: This funny poem by Kenn Nesbitt is about a cat who builds himself a catapult to fly around the house he lives in.

Zangadoo Kangaroo and the Mysterious Boomerang: This book by Karin Lee is about the adventures of the young, soft-hearted kangaroo, Zangadoo, as he tries to find his way home from the Australian outback.

Be Creative!

A. You read about an elf in the poem 'The Elf and the Dormouse'. Can you think of other magical creatures that you have read about in stories and poems?

Make a list of five such creatures and write the magical quality each has in the table below. One is done for you.

Magical creature	Book/story/poem they are from	Magical quality
elf	*The Elf and the Dormouse*	*can fly*

Here are some well-known stories with magical creatures in them to help you: the *Harry Potter* series, *Snow White and the Seven Dwarves, Beauty and the Beast*

B. In the story 'Adventure at the Circus', Neeraj stopped Neha from getting hurt by the speeding motorcycle. Make a 'Thank You' card from Neha to Neeraj using the following steps:

ART INTEGRATION

Step 1: Take plain card paper. Draw or paste a picture on the outside which is related to the theme of the card. You can also write 'Thank You' in big, colourful letters.

Step 2: Write a short message inside the card. Include a greeting and your signature.

Step 3: Make an envelope out of stiff paper. Place your card in the envelope.

C. You learnt the names of four animals and birds from Australia, other than the kangaroo, in the chapter 'Kangaroos'.

Write a note on any one of them. Research the details in your school library or on the Internet. Also draw the animal or bird below he description.

D. You read about Anna Mani's life in 'Anna's Experiments with Weather'. Read about the major events in her life, given in the table. Then complete the timeline by filling in the blanks with the correct years in which the events took place.

Major Events in Anna Mani's life	
Anna goes to work in C.V. Raman's laboratory.	Anna moves to England to study meteorology.
Anna is born in Travancore.	Anna dies in Thiruvananthapuram, Kerala.
Anna retires from the Indian Meteorological Department.	Anna joins the Indian Meteorological Department in Pune.

Timeline

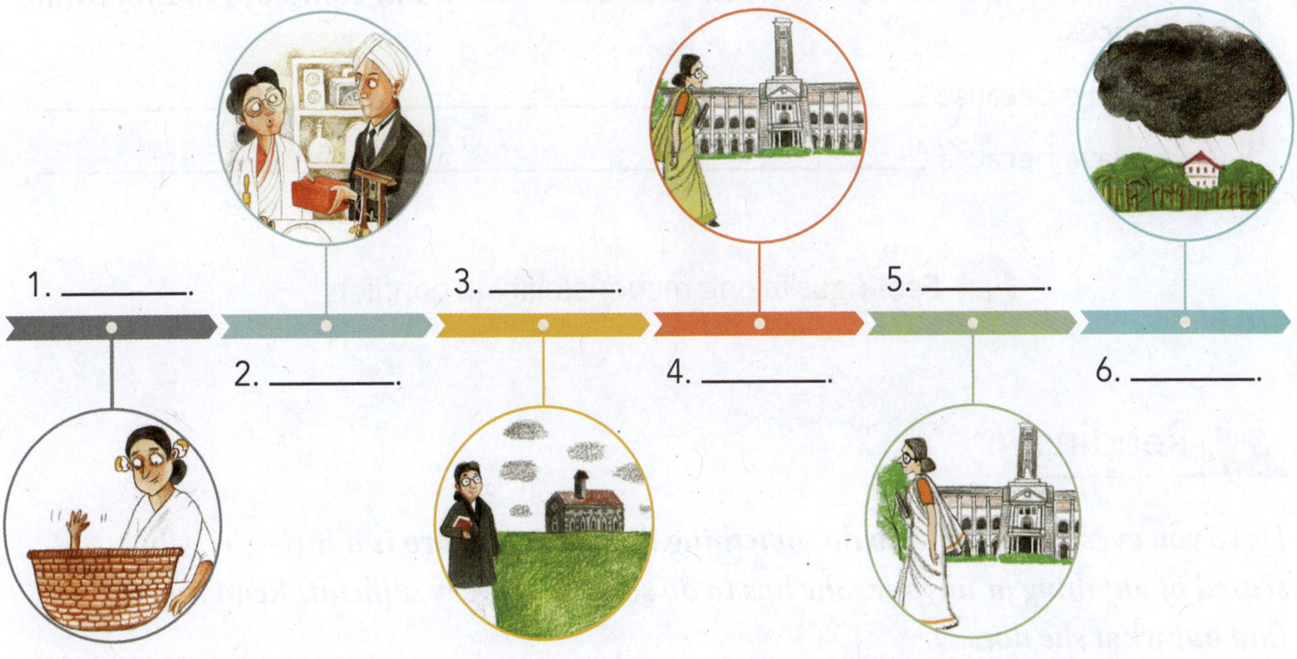

13

Amparo's Journey

Let's Get Started

Look at this word cloud. Circle the words which you think are related to bravery.

bold courageous fearless daring plucky lion-hearted
generous friendly honest kind lucky neat

Bravery is not just about grand actions. An act of bravery is anything that we do which we are afraid of at first, such as standing up to a bully, or sharing our thoughts in class even if we feel shy.

Think of two such times when you have been brave and complete the following sentences.

I am brave because ____________________.

I am brave because ____________________.

HC **Feelings:** Taking responsibility in conflicts

Reading

Have you ever been scared to do something difficult? Amparo is a little girl who is not scared of anything or anyone. She has to do something very difficult. Read this play to find out what she does.

Characters

Amparo: a **stubborn** and determined young girl with a bad **temper**

Pedro, Juan, Miguel, Jose: farmers and Amparo's brothers

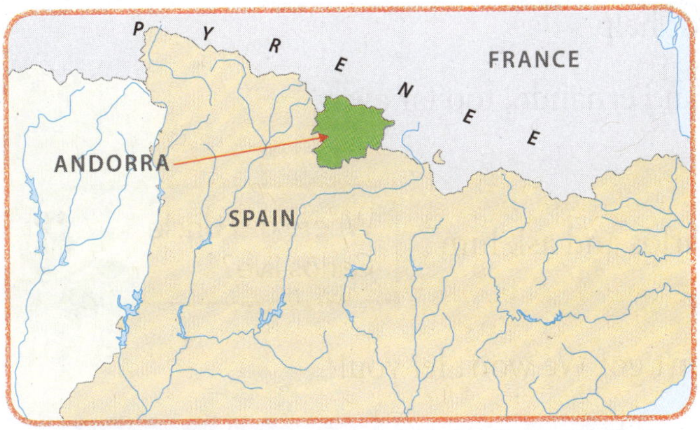

Mountain lynx

Don Ricardo: a proud and rich old man

Carlos: uncle to Amparo and her brothers

El Fanatico: a scary **bandit**

Scene I: Amparo's cottage in San Colombo, a dusty village in Spain, at the foot of the Pyrenees.

[Pedro, Juan, Miguel and Jose are sitting at the table, looking sad. Enter Amparo. She has long, straight hair as black and shiny as a raven's feathers.[1]]

Amparo Huff! I just finished feeding the hens and watering the melons. I've spent all day cooking for you and all you do is sit here like stuffed puppets!

Pedro We are worried, Amparo. We work hard, but the mountains are dry and stony. The crops don't grow well. This year's crop will be poor and we have many bills to pay.

Did You Know? Geography

The Pyrenees mountain range stretches between the countries of Spain and France in Europe, with the tiny Principality of Andorra in between. These mountains are popular for skiing and mountaineering.

stubborn: not wanting to change one's mind

temper: used for someone who gets angry quickly

bandit: dangerous thief

Literary term

1. This is a **simile**. Here, Amparo's hair is being compared to a raven's feathers using the word 'as'.

Miguel If only we could ask Uncle Carlos for help.

Pedro But he lives over the mountains in San Fernando, too far away.

Jose The journey would be too dangerous.

Amparo Nonsense! I'll go and see Uncle Carlos and ask him for help.

Where did Uncle Carlos live?

Pedro, Juan, Miguel, Jose *(together)* You can't go! We won't let you!

Amparo Yes, I can! I will pack a few things and leave tomorrow.

Miguel But there are wild beasts and bandits on the way, and there is no water.

Amparo I will manage. Now eat your dinner and let's hear no more about it.

snarls: makes a sound loudly while showing its teeth

pounce: jump on someone forcefully

Scene II: A dusty road in the mountains. Above the road is a rock, on which stands the Mountain Lynx.

[Enter Amparo. She has a leather flask of water around her waist and a bundle of food tied in a red shawl around her shoulders.]

Did You Know? Science

The mountain lynx, or Iberian lynx is found in southern Europe. It mostly feeds on rabbits. It is the most endangered wild cat species in the world.

Amparo *(looking up)* The sun is quite high in the sky now.

[The lynx ***snarls*** *and shows a set of sharp teeth.]*

Amparo *(angrily)* What are you making all that noise for?

Lynx Aren't you trembling in your shoes, little girl?

Amparo Not at all.

Lynx *(growling angrily)* Yes, you are! Everybody's afraid of me!

Amparo Well, I'm not. So if you don't mind, I have a long journey ahead.

Lynx *(proudly)* I can jump three metres in the air. I can **pounce** on my prey with lightning speed. I can run over snow as fast as...

Amparo Really, how interesting. But I don't have all day to listen to you.

[Amparo walks off, leaving the lynx with his mouth open in ***amazement****.]*

Scene III: Further down the mountain road, at a well.

[Amparo lowers a wooden bucket into the well for water. The sun is beating down hotly.]

amazement: surprise

crossly: angrily and in a bad mood

Amparo What a stroke of luck to find a well here!

[Enter Don Ricardo, a tall man with hair as curly as a sheep's. He wears a rich, grey coat and carries a long walking stick.]

Ricardo *(angrily)* What are you doing?

Amparo *(crossly)* What does it look like I am doing?

Ricardo Don't answer a question with a question, you bold child!

Amparo *(continuing to draw water)* Well, don't shout at me, then. You are scaring the birds away.

Ricardo This is my well! I own it! I am Don Ricardo, the richest man in the –

Amparo Really, how interesting. But I can't stop to listen to you all day. I have a long journey ahead.

[She pulls up the bucket of water, drinks a little, splashes some on her dusty face and fills her flask.]

What did Amparo do with the water from the well?

Ricardo You can't use my well!

Amparo I just have.

[Don Ricardo is stuck for words and watches as Amparo walks off.]

Scene IV: Uncle Carlos' house, in the village of San Fernando

[It is dark and cold. Enter Amparo. She hugs old Carlos, who has come out.]

Carlos My child, I haven't seen you in so long.

Amparo Dear Uncle, we need your help, for we will not have a big harvest this year.

Carlos *(sighing)* I would help you if I could, Amparo, but I have nothing. Every month, El Fanatico and his bandits come down the mountains and take all my money. They will come tomorrow, so you must return home before they arrive.

Amparo Certainly not!

Carlos You must.

Amparo I won't.

Scene V: Next morning, outside Carlos' cottage

[Enter El Fanatico and his gang. He wears a thick black belt and a big red ***sombrero*** *on his head. The others wear big, black boots and have gold rings in their ears. They all carry weapons and look dangerous. Amparo is waiting for them.]*

Amparo *(looking straight at the bandit's dark eyes)* I have been waiting for you.

El Fanatico For me?

Amparo Yes, and I know why you are here.

El Fanatico You do?

Amparo Yes, I do. You are here to pay back all the money you have taken from my Uncle Carlos.

sombrero: hat with a wide brim worn in Mexico and Spain

pesetas: money used in Spain till 2001

lost for words: to be too surprised to speak

El Fanatico I am? You are very brave.

Amparo Yes, I am.

[She quickly pulls out the fat pouch of ***pesetas*** *from the bandit's belt.]*

El Fanatico You can't do that! I am El Fanatico, the cruellest and most wicked bandit in all of Spain...

Amparo Really, how interesting, but I can't stop to listen to you all day. I have a long journey home. But El Fanatico, or whatever they call you, I hope my uncle has seen the last of you.

[Amparo leaves. El Fanatico is ***lost for words****. No one had spoken to him like this before.]*

Scene VI: Outside Amparo's cottage in San Colombo.

[Enter Amparo. Pedro, Juan, Miguel and Jose rush to greet her.]

What did Amparo pull out from the bandit's belt?

Miguel Amparo, you are safe! You are back with us!

Amparo Of course, and I showed that old El Fanatico! He won't trouble Uncle Carlos anymore.

[She gives him the pouch full of pesetas.]

Juan Sister, this will solve all our **woes**! There will even be some money left to replace the broken church bell.

Amparo lived on to become an old lady. She still stays with her brothers in the little village. She feeds the hens and waters her melons and is as ill-tempered as ever.

woes: problems

(Adapted from a story by Gervase Phinn)

Comprehension

Quick Recap

A. Answer these questions.

1. Why were Amparo's brothers worried?
2. Why was the journey going to be dangerous?
3. Who was Don Ricardo? Write the simile used to describe him.
4. Why was Uncle Carlos unable to help Amparo?
5. Give two examples of Amparo's bravery from the play.

B. Read the lines from the play and answer the questions.

1. *I would help you if I could, Amparo, but I have nothing.*
   a. Who is the speaker?
   b. Why can he/she not help Amparo?
   c. What does he/she ask her to do? What is her reply?
2. *I am? You are very brave.*
   a. Who does 'I' refer to?
   b. Who is the speaker talking to?
   c. Why does the speaker call this person brave?

Life Skills and Values bravery

Think and answer.

1. Amparo was able to help her family by doing what she thought was right and not listening to others. Do you think it is right to ask questions if we don't agree with what we are asked to do?

Way with Words

PHRASAL VERBS

A. Complete the sentences with these phrasal verbs from the play. You may have to change the tense in some places.

scare away	ask for	afraid of	run over	shout at

1. The elderly man ______________________ his neighbours who were making a lot of noise.
2. The farmer has placed a scarecrow in his fields to __________ the birds who eat his crop.
3. I thought the car had ______________ a cat, but it was just a plastic bag.
4. I want to _____________ Meesha's help to complete my project, but I know she is busy.
5. Are you __________________ the dark?

SUFFIXES

A **suffix** is a group of letters added at the end of a word to form a new word.

Examples: interest + **ing** = interest**ing** amaze + **ment** = amaze**ment**

B. Choose and add these correct suffixes to form new words.

1. punish_______ (dom/ment/ness)
2. help________ (ful/ship/ish)
3. king________ (ish/ness/dom)
4. sleep________ (ish/y/ful)
5. friend________ (ful/ment/ship)
6. power________ (ness/ful/ish)

Grammar in Use

PRESENT CONTINUOUS TENSE USING HELPING VERBS

Look at the sentence.

Amparo **is guarding** Uncle Carlos cottage.

The verb in bold describes an action that is happening at the time of speaking. It is not yet complete. Such verbs are in the **present continuous tense**.

You will also see that in the present continuous tense, *-ing* words are used along with the helping verbs **is**, **am** and **are**.

Examples: **I am playing** with him.
She **is playing** with him.
They **are playing** with him.

A. Underline the verbs in the present continuous tense in these sentences.

1. Ronit is cleaning his room.
2. The children are playing cricket.
3. I am eating my dinner.
4. We are doing a project on cleanliness.
5. Priya is helping her mother in the kitchen.
6. The dog is chasing the cat.

B. Complete the sentences with the present continuous tense of the given verbs.

1. My friends ________________ to the football match. (go)
2. Ravi ________________ the plants in the garden. (water)
3. Carry an umbrella. It ________________ very heavily. (rain)
4. I ________________ my favourite cartoon show on television. (watch)
5. My mother ________________ pasta today. (cook)
6. The police ________________ after the thief. (run)

Prepositional Phrases

You have learned that prepositions are words that link nouns and pronouns with other words.

Now, look at the sentence.

Amparo got **into the park** after crossing the mountain.

The words in bold form a prepositional phrase.

A **prepositional phrase** tells us something more about a person or an action. They usually start with a preposition and end with a noun or pronoun.

C. Complete the sentences with the correct prepositional phrases.

in the lake	beside the lake	over the river
under the palace	on the table	across the street

1. Maya walked her dog ________________.

2. Ravi is going to swim ________________.
3. The naughty boy sat ________________.
4. The shop ________________ sells pencils and notebooks.
5. There is an old tunnel ________________.
6. The wooden bridge ________________ was built last month.

Study Skills

Spell Check

Look at the word 'JOURNEY' carefully. You will see that you can use the letters in the word to form new words.

Write the following using the letters in the word, 'Journey'.

1. a one-letter word for exclamation ________________
2. a word of two letters ________________
3. a word of three letters ________________
4. a word of four letters ________________
5. a word of five letters ________________

Listening and Speaking

Rising and Falling Intonation in *wh-* Questions

Listen to a set of questions asked by Amparo's brothers, beginning with **where, which, when** and **how**. You will notice that for each question, the voice falls from a higher to a lower level.

Example: **How** can you travel *alone*?
The voice is highest at **How** and lowest at *alone*.

Repeat the questions you have just heard.

In pairs, make ten more questions of your own. Take turns to say them aloud, with your voice falling from a higher to a lower level.

Pen it Down

Amparo solved her family's problems by being brave. Write a paragraph describing a real or imaginary incident when you solved a problem using your intelligence and wit. You can use the these points in your paragraph:

- description of the problem you were facing and how you came to know of it

- how you planned to solve the problem
- people who helped you

Self Assessment

Now I can

- read and understand a play about a girl who bravely faces any difficult situation.
- learn to use suffixes, the present continuous tense and prepositional phrases.
- ask questions with different tones of voice, and write a paragraph on a given topic.

Read More

The Gift of the Crocodile: This tale from Indonesia by Judy Sierra is about a poor girl, Damura, who finds a fairy godmother in old Grandmother Crocodile.

Classic Tales for Children – Bravery Stories: This collection of classic stories by Terry O'Brien shows how people can be courageous in difficult situations.

14

The Land of Fib

Rounak Chawla

Let's Get Started

Do you like stories related to space? What are the things that interest you in such stories: the vastness of space, faraway planets and stars, aliens or strange worlds?

Complete this crossword with the help of the clues given below.

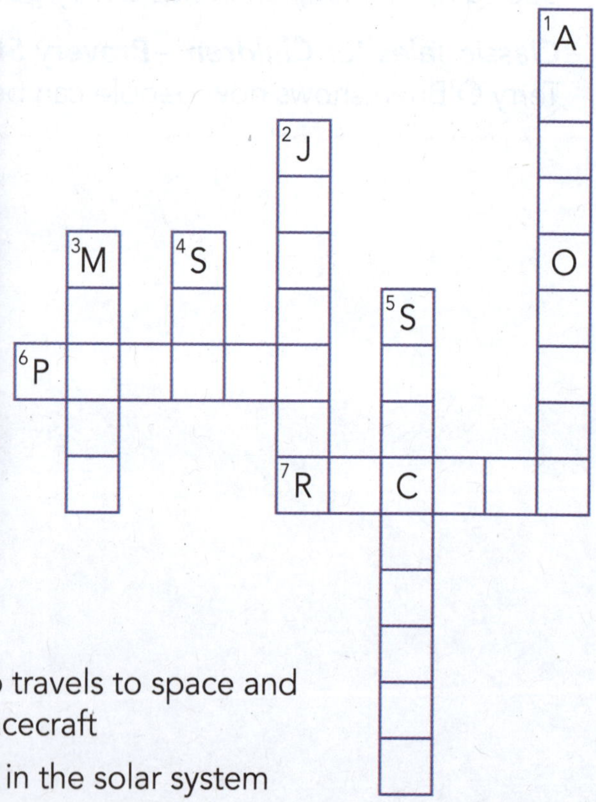

Across:

6. a large, round object in space that moves around a star
7. a spacecraft shaped like a long tube

Down:

1. someone who travels to space and works in a spacecraft
2. largest planet in the solar system
3. the ________ Way is a band of light seen in the night sky. It is made up of a huge number of stars.
4. the star in the middle of our solar system
5. special suit with an air supply, which you wear in space

Learning and Awareness: Difference between knowing and assuming

Reading

We know that it is wrong to lie. But have you thought that it may be better to be truthful than to lie? Read a story about the people of a faraway planet, who lied all the time. Their lives changed when they found that it was more useful to tell the truth.

If you crossed the Chocolate Belt and the rings of the planet of Marriage, and took a left from the Waterless Moon, you would reach the planet of Fib. It was said that a thousand people lived on **Fib**, but you couldn't be sure, because the people of Fib loved to lie.

fib: a lie about something not important

How did the President of Fib look?

They lied at work, they lied for fun, they even dreamed about the lies they would tell the next day.

The President of Fib wore four hats, five watches and very big shoes. When he stepped out of his house, he looked quite like a clown. But when the people of Fib saw him, they always said, 'You look wonderful today, Mr President!'

Did You Know? **Science**

Fib is an imaginary planet. The Earth is a part of the solar system, which consists of the Sun and eight planets. Pluto used to be the ninth planet. But in 2006, scientists decided it was too small to be considered a planet.

The doctors of Fib also lied. There was a common disease on the planet called Bligsis. People who had Bligsis had very smelly feet. But whenever the doctors met people with Bligsis, they would say, 'You are quite healthy!'

The news reporters too lied on TV. 'It will rain today,' the weatherman would say. But it would never rain on that day.

One day, an **astronaut** from Earth was travelling over Fib in his spaceship when the ship suddenly stopped working. It began to **spin rapidly** and crashed on the planet. Thankfully, the astronaut, named John, was not hurt.

astronaut: someone who travels in space

spin: turn around at great speed

rapidly: very quickly

wrecked: destroyed

impress: (here) make someone admire you

appearance: the way one looks

John got out of his **wrecked** ship. The people of Fib had seen the ship crash and came to look at it.

'Who are you?' they asked him.

'My name is Astronaut John. I am from Earth,' he said.

'Earth is far away. How long will you be here?' they asked.

'I don't know,' said Astronaut John. 'My spaceship is broken. I can repair it in a few months.'

They welcomed him to the planet. The President wanted to meet him. He had worn an extra hat and watch that day to **impress** his guest.

Where was Astronaut John from?

The astronaut asked him, 'I'm sorry, sir, but you look terrible. Are you ill?'

Did You Know? Science

In space, astronauts can grow taller by up to two inches within a month. In Russia, astronauts are known as cosmonauts.

The President was shocked. His people said he always looked wonderful when he dressed up. Why did his guest not like his **appearance**? He decided that he would try harder to impress him.

How long would it take to repair the spaceship?

Astronaut John was a special guest on Fib. One day, he was invited to be on the news. Just before his show, the weather presenter was discussing the weather. 'It is going to be a very dry day today,' he said. 'Not a drop of rain.'

John thought this to be very odd. There had been big, black clouds in the sky and it would surely rain. He walked in front of the camera and said, 'Excuse me, I saw big, black clouds when I was coming here. It will definitely rain today.'

The weather presenter was not very happy. He did not like **interruptions**. But it rained the whole day! Many of the citizens of Fib carried their umbrellas to work because of Astronaut John and they were glad that he had spoken the truth.

Why was the weather presenter not happy?

As John was leaving the newsroom, he met the President again. He was wearing only two watches and two hats. 'You are looking much better today, Mr President,' he said.

The President was very happy to be praised. He decided to work a little more to look even better.

A few days later, a little boy called Zog **skinned** his knee. He was in great pain and was crying. But the doctor said, 'To feel better, you have to run to school every day.'

Astronaut John was passing by and he cried, 'What nonsense!'

interruptions: things which temporarily stop an activity

skinned: bruised

wound: injury

heal: become better

pleased: liked

He took a piece of cloth and tied it very tightly around Zog's leg. 'There,' he said. 'Now the **wound** will close and **heal** easily.'

The doctor was not happy. He did not like interruptions either. But because John was a guest, the doctor had to let him do as he **pleased**.

All this time, John was repairing his ship. He even helped the weatherman with his work and the President with his appearance. He did it by simply speaking the truth. The people of Fib were very happy. Their lives were getting better and they understood that it was because John spoke the truth. So, they decided to speak the truth as well.

John repaired his ship in a few months. All the people of Fib came to bid him goodbye. There was the President, who was wearing only one hat and a single watch, with the weather presenter, who never lied about the weather now. Zog was there too. His leg had healed. John waved goodbye to all of them happily and his ship left for Earth.

Comprehension

Quick Recap

A. Number the sentences in the order of the events in the story.

1. The spaceship was repaired after a few months. ☐
2. A few days later, Zog skinned his knee. ☐
3. Astronaut John said that it would rain. ☐
4. Astronaut John's spaceship crashed on the planet of Fib. ☐
5. Many citizens of Fib carried their umbrellas to work. ☐
6. Astronaut John met the President of Fib. ☐

B. Answer the questions.

1. How could a person reach the planet of Fib? How did Astronaut John come to the planet?
2. What did the people of Fib love to do? Give two examples.
3. How did the President of Fib dress?
4. What was the name of the common disease on the planet? What happened to people who had the disease?
5. Why did the President decide to try harder to impress John?
6. What had happened to Zog? How did Astronaut John help him?

C. Read the lines from the story and answer the questions.

1. *'Excuse me, I saw big, black clouds when I was coming here. It will definitely rain today.'*
   a. Who said these words? Where did he say them?
   b. Why did he say these words?
   c. How did it help the people of Fib that day?

Life Skills and Values honesty, self-awareness

Think and answer.

1. Give two examples of the way the doctors on the planet of Fib lied.
2. What did the people of Fib learn from Astronaut John's behaviour? Did it change them?

21ST CENTURY Flexibility

Way with Words

Professions

A. Match the people with the work that they do.

A	B
1. doctor	a. the head of a country or an organisation
2. president	b. collects and reports news for a newspaper or TV
3. astronaut	c. treats people's illnesses
4. weather presenter	d. travels and works in a spacecraft
5. reporter	e. talks about the weather on TV or radio

B. Rewrite the sentences by replacing the underlined words with the words from the box. You may have to add a word in some sentences.

improve	nonsense	weather	odd	extra

1. The <u>climate</u> of the city changes all the time.
2. The man looked quite <u>strange</u> in his green-coloured shoes and orange coat.
3. We can <u>better</u> our lives by speaking the truth.
4. What he is saying is <u>completely senseless</u>.
5. Do you have <u>one more</u> pencil?

Grammar in Use

Past Continuous Tense

Look at this sentence.

An astronaut from Earth **was travelling** on his spaceship.

The verb in bold refers to an action that was happening in the past. The action was ongoing or not yet complete at the time. Such verbs are in the **past continuous tense.**

A. Underline the verbs in the past continuous tense in these sentences.

1. I saw Ronny in the morning. He was running to catch the school bus.
2. Prema was having dinner when the doorbell rang.
3. Everyone was dancing at the party.
4. Did you see Tina yesterday? She was wearing a red dress.
5. Tom was sleeping in his parents' room.
6. Sheila was playing with her sister today.

The Comma

You know that we use the comma (,) to separate three or more words in a list and to organise ideas in a sentence. Before the last word in the list, we add **and** instead of the comma.

Example: Cross the Chocolate Belt**,** the planet of Marriage **and** the Waterless Moon to reach the planet of Fib.

B. Place commas and add and where needed in these sentences.

1. Diya Sonal Priya Sonu are playing in the park.
2. At the fair I rode the giant wheel the toy train the bumper car.
3. My uncle will visit China Japan and Malaysia next month.
4. I had a bowl of cornflakes an egg and half an apple for breakfast.
5. I am playing video games my sister is studying my cousin is reading a book.
6. I want to have a sandwich Parvathi wants to have idlis but Parul wants to eat chapatis.

Study Skills

Use Your Dictionary

Find the word weather in your dictionary. Open the page on which you found the word and answer these questions.

1. What are the words printed at the top of the page on which you found the word 'weather'?
   ____________ ____________
2. Is 'weather' a noun, a verb or an adjective? ____________
3. What are the words just before and after the word 'weather'? Write down their meanings.
   ____________ ____________
   ____________ ____________
4. Write the meaning of the word 'weather'. ____________
5. Is 'weather' a singular or a plural word? ____________

Listening and Speaking

A. There are some questions whose answer is always either 'yes' or 'no'. When we ask such questions, our voice slowly rises while speaking.
Listen to some yes/no questions carefully and practise saying them aloud in class. Then, write two yes/no questions of your own. In pairs, say them aloud in class.

B. Play a fun game in class to create stories using a set of words.

Your teacher will divide the class into five groups. When the teacher says 'start', a student in the group will write the first word that comes to his/her mind on a piece of paper. Then, the next student in the group will write another word beginning with the last letter of the first word. This should continue until everyone in the group has written a word. The following is an example of a set of words created in this way:

colou**r** – **r**unnin**g** – **g**ame**s** – **s**k**y** – **y**ellow

Narrate the story your group creates with their set of words. Every student in the group must say at least one sentence.

Pen it Down

21ST CENTURY Communication

Imagine that you are the boy, Zog. Write a letter to your friend Zoey who lives on another planet, describing how life on Fib changed after Astronaut John showed that that it was better to speak the truth.

You can mention the following points in your letter:

- life on Fib before and after Astronaut John's visit
- an example of how speaking the truth helped you

Self Assessment

Now I can

- read and understand a story on why we should always speak the truth.
- learn that we should always be ready to help others.
- match professions with their meanings, use the past continuous tense, and the comma.
- listen to and ask *yes/no* questions, play a game on creating stories, and write a letter.

Read More

The Adventures of Pinocchio: This book by Carlo Collodi is about a naughty but good-hearted puppet called Pinocchio whose nose grew longer each time he lied.

George Washington and the Cherry Tree: This story by Parson Weems is about the young George Washington, who was not afraid to tell his father the truth about chopping down the latter's favourite cherry tree.

15

The Land of Counterpane

Robert Louis Stevenson

Let's Get Started

To keep ourselves fit and avoid falling sick, it is important to play sports or do some sort of physical activity.

Match each picture and exercise type to its description.

Exercise		Description
1. aerobics		a. This ancient Chinese form is also a martial art. Crowds of people gather in open spaces to perform slow movements that help them relax.
2. zumba		b. Created for the US Air Force in the 1960s, this form is now performed with music. It keeps the heart and lungs healthy.
3. yoga		c. Named after the German doctor who invented it, this activity uses gym equipment like exercise balls, wires and mats. It makes our spine and back strong.
4. tai chi		d. This Colombian fitness activity combines salsa dance with fast exercises. It helps people lose weight in a healthy manner.
5. pilates		e. This ancient Indian form includes breathing exercises, *asanas* or positions and meditation. It is popular worldwide now.

HC **Feelings:** Addressing the core human desire for happiness

Reading

What did you do the last time you fell ill and could not go to school? Read this poem about a sick boy who spends his day at home playing with his toys.

When I was sick and lay a-bed,
I had two pillows at my head,
And all my toys beside me lay
To keep me happy all the day.

And sometimes for an hour or so
I watched my **leaden** soldiers go,
With different uniforms and **drills,**
Among the bedclothes, through the hills;

And sometimes sent my ships in fleets
All up and down among the sheets;
Or brought my trees and houses out,
And planted cities all about.

I was the giant great and still
That sits upon the pillow-hill,
And sees before him, **dale** and plain,
The **pleasant** land of **counterpane.**

leaden: (here) made of lead

drills: exercises

dale: valley

pleasant: lovely

counterpane: a thick bedcover

Where did the young boy send his ships sometimes?

Did You Know? History

Tin soldiers, ships and trains were some of the most popular toys for children when the poem was written. But only the very rich could buy them.

About the poet

Robert Louis Stevenson (1850–1894) was a Scottish writer and poet best known for his book, *Treasure Island*. He was often sick as a child and spent many winters in bed in his imaginary world, with books as his closest friends.

Comprehension

Quick Recap

A. Match the following to make meaningful sentences.

A	B
1. The boy watched the lead soldiers	a. marched through the hills.
2. The toy soldiers	b. for an hour.
3. The boy felt happy	c. because he was sick.
4. The little boy was in bed	d. the pillow against which he was resting.
5. The hill was actually	e. when his toys were with him.

B. Read the lines from the poem and answer the questions.

1. *All up and down among the sheets;*
   Or brought my trees and houses out,
   And planted cities all about.
   a. What does the line, 'All up and down among the sheets' mean?
   b. What did the boy send 'up and down among the sheets'? How did he actually do so?
   c. What do the words 'planted cities' mean? With what did the boy 'plant' his cities?

2. *I was the giant great and still*
   That sits upon the pillow-hill,
   a. Who is 'I' in the sentence?
   b. Explain the phrase 'pillow-hill'.
   c. What could the person see in front of him?

Life Skills and Values

imagination, contentment

Think and answer.

1. What did the boy imagine the lead soldiers were doing?
2. Who does the boy think himself to be? Why do you think he does so?
3. Where do you think the land of counterpane is? How do you think the boy was able to change his sick bed into the land of counterpane?

21ST CENTURY Flexibility

Way with Words

ADJECTIVES

A. Write suitable adjectives of your own to describe these nouns from the poem.

1. ____________ pillows	4. ____________ day	7. ____________ ships
2. ____________ toys	5. ____________ uniforms	8. ____________ cities
3. ____________ soldiers	6. ____________ hills	9. ____________ houses

B. Write the words related to nature in the poem.

C. Find five pairs of rhyming words in the poem.

Grammar in Use

MODAL VERBS

You know that modals are helping verbs. The most common verbs of this type are **can**, **may**, **must**, **will** and **should**.

Can is used to express an ability, something that is likely to happen, to offer a suggestion or to ask for permission.

Examples: He **can** imagine that his wooden soldiers are fighting in a battle. (ability)
Can you lend me some toys? (ask for permission)

May is used to express something that is likely to happen and to ask for formal permission.

Examples: The boy **may** go to school tomorrow. (something that is likely to happen)
May I leave the room? (seek formal permission)

Must is used to make a promise or express a necessity.

Example: You **must** try to sleep now as you are sick. (necessity)

Will is an expression of an action that will take place in the future and a solution to a problem.

Examples: The boy **will** build a toy town later. (action that will take place in the future)
We **will** help him to get better. (solution to a problem)

Should is an expression of something that is likely to happen. It is also used to offer advice.

Examples: We **should** join him in his play-acting. (something that is likely to happen)
You **should** read regularly to enhance your imagination. (advice)

A. Complete the sentences with the modals can, may, must, will or should.

1. The school ______________ definitely choose Amit for this year's cricket team.
2. I ______________ make tea, but I don't know how to make coffee.
3. ______________ I go home early today?
4. The sun is shining brightly. It ______________ be very hot outside.
5. We ______________ all exercise in order to keep fit.
6. I saw my eraser on the table a moment ago. It ______________ be somewhere here!
7. ______________ you speak Japanese?
8. If you finish your homework now, you ______________ have time to play later.

Types of Adjectives

You know that adjectives describe nouns. Look at the table to learn about three different types of adjectives.

Types of adjectives	Examples
Adjectives of quality describe a particular quality that someone or something has.	I brought out my **lead** soldiers to play. The boy had a **happy** smile on his face when he saw his **new** toys.
Adjectives of quantity tell us 'how much' of something or someone there is.	I have **many** friends. Setu has **some** money in his bag. Mani likes **all** sports.
Demonstrative adjectives help us to show or point out certain persons or things.	**This** toy ship is mine. **Those** toy trees and houses are yours. **That** doll is Sam's but **these** books are Suman's.

B. Underline the adjectives in the following sentences and write down what type they are.

1. Some people like jackfruit but I don't.
2. This board game has easy rules.
3. Look at that bird. It is so colourful!
4. Arun has a brown dog.
5. Many people were in the stadium.
6. They bought a new house.
7. I am reading an interesting book.

Study Skills

Spell Check

Write sh or ch to complete the words.

1. You can see the big _____ip from the beach.
2. I went _____opping with my mother today.
3. Don't sit on that _____air. It's broken.
4. My favourite indoor game is _____ess.
5. Jeet jumped into the swimming pool with a big spla_____.
6. It was su_____ a hot day today.
7. I want to be a tea_____er when I grow up.
8. Did you _____ut the door when you left the house?

Listening and Speaking

Listen to a funny poem on the way plurals are formed in English. Write the correct plural words in the poem. Then, in pairs, take turns to ask each other the singular form of the words in plural.

Pen it Down

A. How would you spend your time if you had to stay at home on a school day because you were unwell? Would you read a book, play with your toys, or with your brother or sister? Make a list of five things that you would do.

HC **Learning and Awareness:** Momentary and deeper happiness

B. Rewrite the poem you have just read like a story.

Keep these points in mind:

- Use words that we speak in our day-to-day life.
- Replace words like 'a-bed' and 'dale' with simpler ones, such as 'in bed' and 'valley'.
- Rearrange the order of words. For example, 'I was the giant great and still' will be 'I was the great and still giant'.

Self Assessment

Now I can

- read and understand a poem on how imagination can change something ordinary into something enjoyable.
- study modal verbs, identify types of adjectives, and spell words with 'ch' or 'sh'.
- make a list of things to do, and read a poem and rewrite it like a story.

Read More

My Shadow: In this poem by Robert Louis Stevenson, a child talks about his shadow, imagining it as a friend who is always by his side.

Bed in Summer: In this poem, also by Robert Louis Stevenson, a child complains that in summer he has to go to bed while it is still light outside.

16 Emily's Brush with History

Let's Get Started

The remains of Egyptian Pharaohs were kept in pyramids for thousands of years after their death. The Egyptians believed in life after death. Very often, valuables and essentials were buried with them for use in the after life.

Find these words related to Egypt in the word grid and highlight them.

Nile
pharaoh
desert
mummies
pyramids
gold
Sphinx
papyrus

G	O	L	D	A	B	C	D	Q	E	F	G	H	E
X	W	V	U	T	S	R	Q	O	P	O	N	M	M
D	W	E	M	T	P	Y	U	M	I	O	P	A	U
E	H	J	U	L	H	Z	X	M	C	V	B	N	M
S	T	P	M	I	I	P	O	X	A	S	D	F	G
E	Z	H	M	C	N	V	P	A	P	Y	R	U	S
R	U	A	I	O	X	P	A	S	S	D	F	I	G
T	A	R	E	C	T	V	B	H	N	M	Q	W	X
O	U	A	S	P	P	A	S	H	D	F	G	H	J
Z	X	O	V	B	N	P	Y	R	A	M	I	D	S
P	A	H	S	D	F	G	H	J	K	L	Z	U	X
M	Q	O	W	E	R	T	Y	U	I	O	P	A	R
H	J	Y	R	V	V	E	E	N	I	L	E	Y	X
N	M	Y	Q	W	E	R	T	Y	U	I	O	P	A
G	H	J	K	L	Z	X	C	V	B	N	M	Q	W

HC **Learning and Awareness:** Education and knowledge

Reading

Do you ever wonder how people lived thousands of years ago? Read a story about a young girl who feels that thinking about the past is boring. She changes her mind after

travelling back in time to Egypt.

Emily yawned loudly as her Grandma Dorrie told the story of her trip to Egypt and the pharaoh's **tomb**. She and her sister, Carey had heard the same story more times than they could remember.

Grandma looked at Emily **sternly** and said, 'Do you remember how the Egyptians buried their kings and queens in the pyramids with their treasures, Emily?'

What story did Grandma tell Emily and Carey?

tomb: a monument over a grave

sternly: strictly

trillion: one followed by twelve zeroes

spell: words which have magical power

Egyptologist: someone who studies the civilization of old Egypt

Where did the Egyptians bury their kings and queens?

Did You Know? History

Egypt is a country in Africa. It is famous for its pyramids, which are huge triangular structures.

Pharaohs were the rulers of Egypt in the past.

'Who wants to know what dead people did a **trillion** years ago?' asked Emily.

Grandma said nothing, but she looked at Emily and murmured something, as if whispering a **spell**. Emily wondered what she was up to. But no one else had noticed anything.

The next morning Emily awoke to a great crash outside her room. A loud voice cried, 'Wake up, Dorrie! We must be on our way or we will miss our train.'

Emily leaped out of bed and looked around. Her room looked so different. The furniture seemed to be from her grandparents' time. And who was calling for Dorrie? Emily went to put on the clothes laid out on the bed, but they were not hers. The long lace dress was uncomfortable where the lace touched her neck. The shoes had strange buttons that she did not know how to use.

Outside her bedroom door was a man who looked like Great-uncle Silas in the pictures Grandma had shown them.

'What year is it?' she asked him. 'Who are you?'

The man barked a loud laugh. 'Come, Dorrie, we don't have time for silly games. It's the same year it was yesterday, 1922. I am your Uncle Silas, an **Egyptologist**. We are going to Egypt. Now hurry or we will miss our train.'

It had to be a dream, Emily thought, but it seemed so real.

What did the car not have?

Uncle Silas climbed into a car parked outside the house. She climbed in next to him and got another surprise. The car had no seat belts.

fascinated: very interested

skyscrapers: very tall buildings

Soon, they stopped outside a building that looked like a shopping complex. Inside, Emily found that it was a train station. She watched the people in old-fashioned clothes as they hurried back and forth. She was scared and **fascinated** at the same time.

From the train, Emily looked out of the window. There were no **skyscrapers**, only some tall buildings of brick or stone.

Then, Emily found that they were in Cairo, the capital city of Egypt.

As Emily and her uncle walked through the narrow lanes of the city, she saw many old houses with grand balconies. She decided to ask Uncle Silas later about the people who must live there.

The next day, Emily and Uncle Silas went to see the pyramids in a nearby town called Giza. Emily could not believe how grand they were! They entered one of the tombs through a narrow pathway and reached the centre of the building where the mummy was kept.

The mummy was covered from head to toe in brown cloth. There was a mask over its face. Eyes were painted on it, making it look alive. There were beautiful patterns on the case in which it was kept.

Emily felt a little sorry for the mummy. It had once been a living person. Now it was on display, to be looked at by strangers.

Uncle Silas said, 'Can you imagine how intelligent

What did the mummy look like?

the people of **ancient** Egypt were, Dorrie? Centuries before us, they learnt to build huge pyramids and **preserve** their dead.'

'But it won't last long if it is kept in the open,' he sighed. 'The mummies are so old that they will fall apart under these conditions.'

Emily felt very sad at the thought.

She was about to touch the mummy when she felt someone shaking her. It was Carey. 'Emily,' she exclaimed. 'I was trying to wake you up for such a long time! What happened?'

A loud voice from behind Carey said, 'Oh, nothing's happened to Emily. She was only sleeping soundly.'

Grandma Dorrie smiled down at Emily. She smiled back. When they were alone, Emily asked, 'You sent me back in time to teach me a lesson, didn't you? The past isn't just about boring dates and facts. It's about real people.'

Grandma Dorrie **ruffled** Emily's hair.

'The next time, you have to teach me the spell that you used too,' Emily said.

Did You Know? Science

Egyptians could keep the bodies of their dead in good condition for thousands of years using a special process. The preserved body was called a 'mummy'.

ancient: very old

preserve: keep something in good condition

ruffled: ran one's hand through someone's hair

What did Emily want to learn the next time?

Comprehension

Quick Recap

A. Answer the questions in a few lines.

1. Why did Grandma Dorrie look sternly at Emily?
2. What woke Emily up the next morning?
3. Why was Emily surprised when she looked around her room?
4. Which were the two cities that Emily and her uncle visited? What did Emily see in each city?
5. Why did Emily feel sorry for the mummy?
6. What did Uncle Silas say about the people of ancient Egypt?
7. Who sent Emily to Egypt? How did the person send her there?
8. What did Emily ask Grandma Dorrie to teach her?

B. Read the lines from the story and answer the questions.

1. *'We must be on our way or we will miss our train.'*
   a. Who said these words and to whom?
   b. Where were they going and why?
   c. How did they travel to the train station?

2. *'But it won't last long if it is kept in the open.'*
   a. Where was the speaker when he said these words?
   b. What is called 'it' in the given line? What did 'it' look like?
   c. Why wouldn't 'it' last long in the open?

3. *'I was trying to wake you up for such a long time!'*
   a. Who said these words and to whom?
   b. What was the sleeping person about to do when she woke up?
   c. What did another person say in reply to these words? Who was she?

Life Skills and Values — learning from the past

Think and answer.

1. Do you think Emily's opinion about history changed after her visit to the pyramid?
2. Write two differences that Emily noticed between her own world and the past.

21ST CENTURY Information Literacy

Way with Words

Compound Words

You know that we can combine two words to form new words.
Examples: grand + parents = grandparents
sky + scraper = skyscraper
These new words are called **compound words**.

A. Match the words in the two columns to make meaningful words.

A	B
1. weather	a. words
2. key	b. flower
3. hand	c. man
4. sun	d. flies
5. pass	e. bag
6. fire	f. board

B. Now, complete the sentences with the words you have made.

1. I cannot find the letter 'l' on the ________________.
2. The ________________ raised its face to the sun.
3. The ________________ said that there would be heavy rain tomorrow morning.
4. I saw the ________________ glow in the dark.
5. The blue ________________ is a gift from my sister.
6. I have so many ________________ that I keep forgetting them.

Collocations

Some words are often used together in English. **Examples:** fall asleep, lie down.
Such word groups are called **collocations**.

C. Complete the sentences with the given words. Then, circle the words which are used together.

lies	got	have	came	do

1. Arun didn't take his raincoat and ________________ wet in the rain.
2. My grandmother ________________ down for an hour after lunch.
3. Gogol ________________ first in a swimming competition after he stopped eating cheese all the time.

4. In summer, I ________________ a bath in the evening.
5. ________________ your best in the exam.

Grammar in Use

Joining Sentences with *Who*

Look at the sentences.

Outside her bedroom door was a man.
The man looked like Great-uncle Silas.

The two sentences can be joined using **who** in the following way:

Outside her bedroom door was a man **who** looked like Great-uncle Silas.

A. Join these sentences using who.

1. The police finally caught the thief. The thief had robbed four houses.
2. I went to the doctor. The doctor also treats my brother.
3. I wish I could meet King Tut. King Tut was called the boy king of Egypt.
4. My mother went to the bookseller. The bookseller sells books by my favourite writers.
5. I love reading books by Enid Blyton. Enid Blyton wrote *The Faraway Tree*.

Punctuation: Capital Letters and Full Stop

A **capital letter** is used at the beginning of a sentence and for proper nouns.

Examples: **W**e must be on our way or we will miss our train.
(at the beginning of a sentence)
Then, **E**mily found that they were in **C**airo, the capital city of **E**gypt.
(for proper nouns)

A **full stop** is used to denote the end of a sentence.

Example: She was about to touch the mummy when she felt someone shaking her.

B. Rewrite the paragraph using punctuation marks where needed. You may need to use capital letters for some of the words.

sonali went to london last summer with her family she had a lot of fun sightseeing visiting relatives and shopping she visited the tower of london buckingham palace and many museums she bought two dresses a pair of shoes and chocolates for herself she asked her father to take her to london again

Study Skills

Pronounce Well

Read the two words in the table aloud. Did you notice that the letters **-ng-** are pronounced differently in each word?

Now, read the words in the box aloud and write them in the correct columns.

ginger	sing	bangle	stranger	long
tongue	manger	swing	angel	change

danger	king

Listening and Speaking

Listen to a conversation between two people who have met for the first time.
Then, imagine the following situation: You visited a pyramid in Egypt during the summer holidays. When you entered the tomb, the mummy suddenly came to life and started talking with you. What do you think it would say?

In pairs, enact a conversation between yourself and the mummy.
Use some of the questions you have just heard.

(Remember, all the questions you ask the mummy should be in the past tense.)

Pen it Down

21ST CENTURY Creativity

If you had the chance to travel to any place you wanted for a holiday, where would you go and why? Write a paragraph on the topic, giving reasons for your choice.

You should include the following points in your paragraph:

- the place and its location. **Example:** Mcleodganj, Himachal Pradesh
- how you can reach the place
- the activities it offers
- the reasons why you want to visit it

Self Assessment

Now I can

- read and understand a story that shows us that history is about real people and not just about facts and figures.
- form compound words and collocations, join sentences with 'who' and use the different punctuation marks.
- practise the different pronunciations of words with 'ng', enact a conversation, and write a paragraph on a given topic.

Read More

Daughter of the Nile: This book by Kristiana Gregory is an imaginary diary of the famous Egyptian queen, Cleopatra, when she was a young girl. She writes about life in Egypt, the evil plots in the royal palace and her escape to Rome.

Tales of Ancient Egypt: This book by Roger Lancelyn Green has stories about the gods and goddesses of ancient Egypt, such as Amen-Ra, Isis and Osiris. It also includes tales of magic and adventure from Egypt.

17

An Animal's Prayer

Rehana Ali

SUSTAINABLE DEVELOPMENT GOALS

13 CLIMATE ACTION

Let's Get Started

The United Nations Sustainable Development Goal 13 is about climate action. It says that we must bring down the harmful effects of climate change. One way to do this is by stopping our seas and oceans from becoming more polluted.

Imagine that you were building a sand castle on the beach. Suddenly a turtle crawls up and starts to speak to you about how humans dirty the sea. Complete the dialogue.

You : Hi, Mr Turtle. ____________________

Turtle: ____________________

You: ____________________

Turtle: But humans ____________________

You: How do you think ____________________

Turtle: ____________________

You: ____________________

Turtle: If humans would ____________________

You: I am ____________________

Turtle: ____________________ Thank you.

HC **Learning and Awareness:** Recognizing characteristics and intrinsic nature of entities

Reading

Have you wondered what animals would say to us if they could speak? Read a poem in which animals talk about the way human beings cause harm to their own planet

while animals live in sync with Nature.

As **stubborn** as a donkey,
As **frisky** as a hare,
As funny as a monkey,
As angry as a bear.

As fat as an elephant,
Sly as a fox can be,
As **thick-skinned** as a rhino,
Cruel as a shark at sea.

We humans have a habit,
Of making such careless talk,
Being rude we say is '**catty**',
And an angry shout a 'bark'.

Let us see what animals,
Have to say about us too,
Their comments would surely surprise,
The likes of me and you.

'We animals may be lazy,
And like to sleep all day,
It's true we only think of food,
In every possible way.

'But we never cheat our friends,
We never kill for **game**,
We never grab another's wealth,
For that is such a shame.

'We wage no war on nature,
By cutting trees more and more,
Or building ugly dams to stop,
The rivers as they flow.

stubborn: not wanting to change

frisky: full of energy

sly: cunning

thick-skinned: not caring about unkind remarks

catty: (here) cat-like

game: (here) wild animals or birds which are hunted by people

What do animals think about all day?

pollute: to add dirty or harmful substances to land, air or water

grime: dirt

Where do humans lock up their fellow beings?

'We do not lock up fellow beings,
In ugly prison cells,
We don't **pollute** the air we breathe,
With smoke and **grime** as well.'

And at the end of every day,
All birds and beasts pray thus,
'God, for making me an animal,
Thank you very much.'

Comprehension

Quick Recap

A. Answer the questions in a few lines.

1. Name the sea creature mentioned in the poem and the adjective used to describe it.
2. Mention two things that animals like to do.
3. According to animals, how do human beings treat each other?
4. With what do people pollute the air around them?
5. What do all animals do at the end of the day?

B. Read the lines from the poem and answer the questions.

1. *We humans have a habit,/Of making such careless talk*
   a. About whom do human beings talk carelessly?
   b. Give two examples of 'careless talk'.
2. *We wage no war on nature*
   a. Who is the speaker in these lines?
   b. What does the phrase 'wage war' mean?
   c. Who wages war on nature and in what way?

Life Skills and Values — knowledge and awareness

Think and answer.

1. The animals describe themselves as lazy creatures, who like to eat and sleep all day. Do you think these are bad qualities in an animal?
2. Write the names of the animals mentioned in the poem in the order of their size.

21ST CENTURY Critical Thinking

Way with Words

Similes

Look at this sentence.

The man is <u>as stubborn as a donkey</u>.

You know that the underlined phrase is a **simile**.

A. Choose the correct word to complete the similes in each sentence.

1. Is there anything to eat? I am as hungry as a ________. (horse/hunter/cow)
2. Gita stayed as cool as a ________ during the fire. (tomato/cucumber/apple)
3. The thief was as quiet as a ________ as he slipped into the house. (feather/mouse/baby)
4. You can't cheat Sam. He is as cunning as a ________. (fox/donkey/bull)
5. By the time Lee Hong turned a hundred years old, he was as blind as a ________. (bee/lion/bat)

Animals and Their Young

B. Complete the sentences with the names of the young ones of some common animals.

1. The k____________ wanted to play with a ball of wool.
2. The c____________ touched its mother's trunk with its own.
3. The ____________b was beginning to grow its first coat of wool.
4. The c____________ was surprised by its mother's roar.
5. The t____________s swam after the frog in the shallow pool.

Grammar in Use

Types of Adverbs

An **adverb** is used to describe a verb, an adjective or another adverb.

Adverbs of manner indicate how an action took place.

Examples: Animals do not treat each other **cruelly**.
We humans have a habit of talking **carelessly**.

Adverbs of place indicate where the action took place.

Examples: We looked for the hare **everywhere**.
The elephant waited **there** for the bear.

Adverbs of time indicate when the action took place.

Examples: The animals will say that they have not seen such human beings **before**.
Humans are **still** preying on animals.

A. Tick the adverbs of manner, underline the adverbs of place and circle the adverbs of time in these sentences.

1. Please handle the glass jar carefully.
2. Jack's hat was lying here on the shelf.
3. Henna politely asked for a spoon.
4. Ananya is playing with her dog outside the house.
5. Shayla's flight arrived late.
6. Raghu slept early as he was tired.
7. They studied quietly in the library.
8. I searched for the book everywhere but didn't find it.

APOSTROPHE

Look at this sentence.

We never grab another's wealth.

Here, the phrase **another's wealth** means 'wealth that belongs to another (person)'.

We use an **apostrophe** (') to show that something belongs to or is related to someone.

We add **'s** to a singular noun to show possession.

Example: We played with the girl**'s** doll.

We add only **'** to a plural noun that end with **s**.

Example: The boys' hostel is just across the road.

We add **'s** to a plural noun that does not end with **s**.

Example: Santa had come to deliver the children**'s** gifts.

If a name ends in **s**, then possession can be shown either way.

Example: We went over to James'/James**'s** house.

B. Add an apostrophe in the right place and rewrite the sentences. One is done for you.

1. *The book that belongs to Sonia is lost.* *Sonia's book is lost.*
2. The dress that belongs to my sister does not fit me.

3. The beak of the bird is sharp and green in colour.
4. The family of Suresh is going on a holiday.
5. The tail of the horse is very long.
6. The watch that belongs to my uncle is very expensive.
7. The growl of a tiger nearby scared the villagers.
8. The game of the children ends at six o'clock.

Study Skills

Use Your Dictionary

You know that many words have different meanings even though they are spelt the same. Write two different meanings of the word wage using your dictionary and make sentences with them.

1. wage - ____________________
____
2. wage - ____________________
____

Listening and Speaking

What can you do to protect the environment in your own way? In pairs, think of two ways and discuss them in class.

You can think of the following points:

- how to increase the number of trees in your city
- how to lessen air pollution
- how to save water
- how to reduce the use of plastic
- how to reduce waste at home and generate less garbage

Pen it Down

The poem talks about the harm caused by the thoughtless actions of people. But human beings are also kind to people and animals.

Complete this imaginary dialogue between an animal and a human being, who suddenly meet in a forest. The animal is talking about the faults in people, while the human being is pointing out the good qualities of people. At the end, add two to three sentences for each speaker.

Human: Hello there! Who are you?

Animal: Hello, dear human. I am ______________, the tiger. I live in this ______________.

Human: Oh! A ______________, are you? Do you eat __________? Please don't __________.

Animal: Of course not! I don't ______________ and most ______________. We don't harm other beings unless ____________________________. We are not like humans.

Human: Yes, but ______________. Some of us do eat meat and fish but we also ______________________________. We keep them as pets. They are like our ______________.

Animal: You care for ______________, but what about ______________? You cut down forests and destroy ______________. Animals have no ______________ ______________. That is why they enter towns and cities and ______________.

Human: It is true that we humans ____, but we also ____.

Animal: Hmph! We also have to survive, but we don't ______________________________ ______________________________. In fact, we ______________________________.

Self Assessment

Now I can

- read and understand a poem on what an animal might think of our world.
- use similes, the different types of adverbs and the apostrophe correctly.
- speak on a given topic, and write an imaginary dialogue.

Read More

When the Animals Saved Earth: This Middle-Eastern fable, retold by Alexis York Lumbard, is about a faraway island where only animals live. Their lives change when humans settle on the island and put them to work.

Lightfoot the Deer: This book by Thornton W. Burgess is about a brave and gentle deer who is hunted by a man with a gun. The deer is helped by the animals of the Green Forest.

Be Creative!

A. You read the poem 'Kangaroos' and you know that the kangaroo is the national animal of Australia. Every country has a national animal. For example, the elephant is the national animal of Thailand.

Choose the national animal of any country. Work in groups and write five interesting facts about the animal. Arrange the facts in the following pattern and draw a picture of the animal beside it.

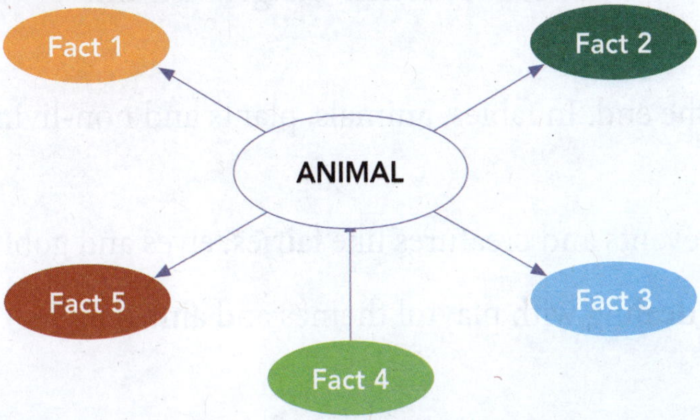

B. In the play 'Amparo's Journey', you learnt about a brave girl who makes a journey alone.

Write a short paragraph about a time when you had to travel without your parents or when you stayed somewhere without them (with relatives/friends/classmates). Describe what you felt and experienced. It could also be an imaginary journey.

C. In 'Emily's Brush with History', you saw how Grandma Dorrie cast a magic spell to send Emily back in time to Egypt.

Write a paragraph about an experience related to magic using the following clues:

you visit a museum with friends ... enter a room ... puppets on display ... your friends move on ... you stay behind ... door closes suddenly ... puppets come to life ... they talk and dance ... you are fascinated ... after a while, your friends join you ... you tell them about your experience ... they don't believe you ... you show them an object which surprises them

Literary Genres and Terms

Literary Genres

The stories which you have read in this book are of various types. The following are some common types of stories.

An **adventure** is a type of story or book which has a lot of action, danger, risk and excitement.

A **fable** is a story with a moral lesson at the end. In fables, animals, plants and non-living things often speak like humans.

A **fairy tale** is a story which has magical events and creatures like fairies, elves and goblins.

Light verse is humorous poetry, usually dealing with playful themes and aimed at amusing the reader.

A **descriptive poem** describes in detail the subject of the poem rather than telling a story or talking about feelings.

A **short story** narrates a tale that is only a few pages long.

Non-fiction is a type of prose that is based on real events rather than imaginary ones.

A **folktale** is a story common among people who come from the same background. It is usually passed on in the form of an oral tale.

A **graphic story** is a story told through words and pictures arranged in a sequence, with dialogues given in speech bubbles.

An **autobiography** is a type of story or book in which the author writes about stories and events from his/her own life.

Literary Terms

Literary terms include common figures of speech. These are the various techniques writers use to convey their message.

A **simile** is a figure of speech in which someone or something is compared to a very different person or thing using 'as' or 'like'. **Example:** He is as brave as a lion.